HOW NOT TO PRAY

HOW NOT TO PRAY

A Fresh Look at Prayer

Jeff Lucas

First published 2003 by Spring Harvest Publishing Division
and Authentic Lifestyle

09 08 07 06 05 04 03   7 6 5 4 3 2 1

Authentic Lifestyle is an imprint of Authentic Media
PO Box 300, Carlisle, Cumbria CA3 0QS
and PO Box 1047, Waynesboro, GA 30830-2047, USA
www.paternoster-publishing.com

British Library Cataloguing in Publication Data

A catalogue record for this book is available from the British
Library

1-85078-452-3

There are several quotations included in the text for which there are
incomplete biographical details as they could not traced, if we are supplied
with these details we will include them when the book is reprinted

Cover design by David Lund
Printed in Great Britain by Cox and Wyman, Reading

Dedication

To Ben, who loves to worship, and who
is himself a wonderful answer to prayer.
Welcome to our family.

Contents

Introduction

Well done you!...

Let me begin by offering you, dear reader – or potential reader – a word of warm, hearty congratulation. Well done – because you have picked up a book that includes the word 'prayer' in its title. This was rather brave of you; I normally run from them myself, because I find it difficult to cope with the heady mixture of inspiration and intimidation that usually mugs me in turn whenever I read about prayer.

The books on prayer that thrill and terrify me are often well written, carefully researched, meticulously punctuated and peppered with multitudinous Bible references. My problem is that people who are quite good at praying usually write books about prayer. A few pages, and I feel like a twenty-five stone arthritic in a Manchester United shirt kicking a ball around with David Beckham. Not a super feeling.

Intimidation runs to dangerous levels when the book talks about any kind of *extended* prayer. By extended, I mean, well, anything over fifteen minutes or so.

I pore over the biographical details of some jolly chap who followed Jesus five hundred years before anything was on television, who passed his days in thrilled solitude, and who perhaps was in the habit of crawling into a hollow log for three days of uninterrupted intercession. This log burrowing is supposed to cheer me up and encourage me to head for the woods myself, but instead, I immediately feel the need for a conference call with the Samaritans. I wouldn't last thirty minutes in the bowels of an intercessory tree, and the only 'deep ministry' that would result would be the wood lice investigating my underwear. Start talking casually about 'the devotional life', and I get that feeling that I used to experience when my school report included the comment in red Biro: 'could do better'.

Just the other day, I bumped into William Penn's description of the great Quaker leader, George Fox. It was both awe-inspiring and daunting

> But above all, he excelled in prayer. The inwardness and weight of his spirit, the reverence and solemnity of his dress and behaviour, and the fewness and fullness of his words, have often struck even strangers with admiration, and they used to reach others with consolation. The most awful, living, reverent frame I ever felt or beheld, I must say, was in his prayer...

There is no doubting the huge heart of Fox; and he is a worthy model for those who aspire to go beyond superficiality and trite spirituality to find a deeper walk with God. But then I read the account again, and I am overshadowed by the man's sheer greatness. I give up, drowned by the huge tidal wave of his godliness. As for Fox's few words, I find that all too often they gush out of me with the speed and control of Niagara Falls. And his weighty spirit? Mine's been to Weight Watchers.

As an *Every Day with Jesus* fan, I confess that often it's *Every other day with Jesus*. I go through seasons when I wish that there was a devotional product available called

Once in a while with God. Every year on New Year's Eve, I enter into solemn vows, planning to read my Bible right through. I invariably come unstuck in the gall bladders of Leviticus or the family trees of Chronicles and Kings. I'm currently developing a *Read through the Bible in three hundred years* course...

Then there's my problem with this trend that writers of books about prayer often seem continuously to inhabit an emotional, spiritual land called *Utter Certainty!* This bold, superlative location is a doubtless zone; awkward questions about pain, suffering, and why I broke down last month (just after leaving the RAC) have no place there. I do have occasional day trips to *Utter Certainty!* and it's a great resort. Fog is banished in that place, and every detail of the landscape is drawn in bold, solid lines; I really would quite like to make *Utter Certainty!* my permanent home.

But then there are some days – more than I'd like to admit – when I find myself meandering off, like the somewhat dull sheep-like person that I am, to camp out for a while on the chilly, bleak moors of an inhospitable location called *Where am I and where has God gone?* Treacherous quicksands threaten to suck me under forever and familiar landmarks seem to disappear in the swirling mists. It's a place that's about as warm and friendly as the set of *The Hound of the Baskervilles*. I stumble on, hoping for a welcome light to lead me home. The bitter cold snaps at my fingers and toes, and I long for a guide – or God – to get me out of that wasteland.

All this is said, dear reader, to let you know that I write this, not as an expert on life, on all things spiritual, but as a bumpkin doing his best – sometimes – to be a follower and an apprentice of Jesus. Get the message? Put your intimidation away: this book is not penned by an expert on the subject of prayer.

Perhaps you're still not convinced, so I'll say more.

I fall asleep when I pray. I'm inconsistent when it comes to worship. Occasionally I find myself over-whelmed with praise for God, which flows out of me in spontaneous thanksgiving, a gushing well. And sometimes that worship is diminished to the *plop plop plop* of a dripping tap, no flowing stream now but just the last dregs of rust-stained water, clogged in the pipes. Being of charismatic persuasion, I sometimes speak in tongues when I pray, believing this to be a language of the Holy Spirit. This too is erratic; sometimes allowing me to sing out a serenade to God without intelligible words, a passionate offering, intimate, loving the Divine Lover. At other times, this practice leaves me feeling that I am chanting some bizarre charismatic mantra that has got about as much passion as the recitation of a railway timetable.

Okay, enough already. Perhaps I've overdone things, and you're now wondering what on earth I could say that could help you to pray. Why should you buy this book? Well, first of all, let me say without hesitation that it is God's perfect will that you make this purchase. (Only kidding.) Seriously, I'd like to invite you to join me and the crowd who wander up to Jesus and say, perhaps somewhat pathetically, 'Lord, teach us how to pray.' I'd like to ask you to grab a coffee, pull up a chair, and take a good look at this business of praying, because I remain convinced that Jesus wants us to pray. He assumed three things of his followers in the Sermon on the Mount: that we would pray, fast, and give help to the poor, and wants to help us to move forward in our praying.

Some of us don't pray much, and it's not because dark and diabolical forces are camped out in our bathrooms, conspiring to stamp out our praying. Rather, the enemy of our praying is what is contained between our ears.

Strongholds, castles of thoughts have been steadily built in our minds over the years, subtle and obvious deceptions that militate against our praying and defeat us before we start. The shorthand word that I'd like to use for these strongholds is *myths*. Perhaps some of them truly are engineered in hell; but for the most part, we have built our own castles. That's why some churches don't require any spiritual attack whatsoever in order to render them ineffective: all the seeds of their impotency are deeply planted in the individual and collective consciousness of their members. They are brought down, defeated by their own thinking, hence the title of Clive Calver's book of some years ago: *With a Church Like This, Who Needs Satan?*

So I'd like to examine a few of those myths, and see if we can clear the rubble of our minds. In doing so, perhaps we will find ourselves praying better – even later today, or tomorrow maybe. The basis for our journey is the Lord's Prayer – or the disciples' prayer – or the Lord's model prayer. Hey, I don't really care what you call it, it's the familiar one that reminds you of the smell of stale school milk that begins 'Our Father' – and you'll remember that it goes like this: (don't skip over this bit please... caught you...)

Our Father in heaven,
hallowed be your name,
your kingdom come,
your will be done
on earth as it is in heaven.
Give us today our daily bread.
Forgive us our debts,
as we also have forgiven our debtors.
And lead us not into temptation,
but deliver us from the evil one. (Mt. 6:9-13)

Okay, let's go. Onward, through the fog.

Jeff Lucas
Somewhere above the Arctic, 2003

1

Believe that you can't pray...

'When you pray...'

Ever find yourself looking around on Sunday morning, during worship, and checking out your fellow congregation? I am an avid student of people, so do this more than I should, with a variety of results. Sometimes I feel a warm trickle of gratitude, as I am thankful for the family of Christians that God has given me – what a fine, fun lot they are!

But most of the time I think that when we survey the home crowd of our local church, we actually feel that everyone is superior to us. Surely, we reason, they've all read Leviticus through twice this morning, and all have an ISDN prayer line, constantly connected at super high speed. Their hearts are, we reason, less likely to be sullied by fear, doubt, lust, anxiety and angst at the size of Doris' hat (whose straw fruit bowl head covering is eclipsing the sun). We alone are the solitary low life types who wrestle with such carnality. The same tendency towards self-dismissal and the feeling that 'I am the only one who can't do this' kicks in quickly when it comes to thinking about prayer...

We can nurse the notion that *everyone else* is adept at praying, but that we have the franchise on failure when it comes to personal spirituality. Crises break out deep inside the heads of people who attend those long prayer meetings to which boredom gives the whiff of penance. After what seems the twentieth hour, even though we've only actually been there for twenty minutes, we risk opening our eyes to take a quick glance at our watches during a numbingly snory prayer. It is then we imagine, with a major flush of inferiority, that everyone else in the place is hurtling along the intercessory information super highway with fluid ease, no trouble with a meandering mind for them, no momentary lapses of concentration threatening their unbroken harmony with heaven, no drifting into wondering what's going to happen in *EastEnders*.

The truth is, we all struggle and that knowledge alone can be liberating. There are no live inhabitants of planet Earth who currently do not have 'flesh' – and the Bible makes it clear that, whatever our great aspirations, the spirit is willing – and the flesh is weak.[1] Struggles in prayer are not symptoms of some creeping spiritual disease in your life, or authentic evidence that confirms your fear that you really are a third class disciple; rather, the difficulty we all face is simply evidence of two facts:

1. We are alive (hence the flesh is operating)
2. Jesus hasn't come back yet (hence we are still struggling)

Spiritually speaking, we are currently on the dark side of the moon, and radio communication is, at best, somewhat patchy. Daily we contend with the 'interference'

---

[1] Mark 14:38

that comes from being in this condition. One day, we will see Jesus with the 20/20 clarity that is eternity, and in that dawning vision everything else will become clear; obscurity and mystery will snap into focus on that bright day. In the meantime, we are those who are peering through grubby double glazing (my paraphrase of 'Now we see but through a glass darkly').[2] To not be able to see it all as we would like should come as no surprise to us. God knows our struggle and the Bible is very candid about our ineptitude. 'We don't know how to pray as we ought'[3] has become one of my favourite Bible verses. Far from condemning us for our half sight and occasional blindness, God recognises the limitations of our current condition. This is the reality for us all and not just for you.

But what about Norman the bionic pray-er?...

... I hear you protest. Perhaps there is one in your church who is a Concorde prayer warrior and seems to be able to soar into spiritual ionospheres, while you chug along in a desperate attempt just to get your ancient prayer bi-plane off the ground. It coughs and splutters and barely lifts its old tyres three feet off the runway; and then it crashes back down again in bone-jarring defeat. Norman zips by you with supersonic, fluid ease...

Yes, there are some people who are *very* good at prayer – and some who have a particular calling to pray. In fact, these are often the ones who write those books about prayer that I mentioned earlier. I read the stories of epic prayer heroes like Rees Howells or John 'Praying'

---

[2] 1 Corinthians 13:12
[3] Romans 8:26

Hyde (good job his last name wasn't 'Mantis') and feel like a prayer David trembling before an intercessory Goliath. But can I put it as bluntly as this? *The stories aren't completely true.* Some biographical writing about prayer is blessedly peppered with sweat, tears and disappointment, balancing them wonderfully. But the fact is that often we only get the edited victory reports, and therefore the victory reports aren't the whole story.

Something similar happens in public meetings when someone shares a blessing that God has given them or some answer to prayer. Am I suggesting that these stories are all embellished or exaggerated? Of course not! With the exception of those rabid evangelistic types who led six million people to Jesus in Sainsburys last Saturday – and that before they'd even got their shopping – most people tell the truth when they talk about their friendship with God. But the sharing usually will only spotlight the *successes* in prayer. Simple limitations of time mean that we don't get to hear about the other prayers that seemed to be met with a stony lack of response from God. We hear about the ecstasy, but little of the agony.

The problem is further compounded in that, in some churches, to say your prayers are not apparently being answered would be considered to be a 'negative confession', a betrayal that would definitely let the side down. Thus, to put it crudely, we often only hear the edited, brighter parts of the story.

Sometimes Norman the bionic prayer warrior will resort to clichés, normally good for squeezing out a few murmured 'Amens' from the congregation, but which leave me baffled. An obvious example can be found in reports of answered prayer. 'Everybody in my office went down with a nasty dose of bubonic plague last week,' cries Norman with gusto. 'The streets were absolutely clogged with hearse carts and the sounds of people screaming "Bring out your dead!" I, Norman, however, did not go down with any nasty boils or plague-like symptoms. The Lord has spared me from this wicked curse. *Isn't the Lord good?'*

Yes, I want to shout, the Lord is good – and I'm delighted, Norman, to hear of your deliverance in the boil department. But is the Lord only *good* when we're spared? Christians died in the unspeakably ugly tragedy that unravelled on our television screens when New York's Twin Towers were devastated by terrorist-steered planes. Was the Lord having an off day – or being *bad* perhaps? I don't believe so. Let's be careful with slogan theology that seems to infer that God is only on form when the sun is shining. Not only will we be disappointed, but others who are trying to find their way home through a rainstorm can get very hurt indeed.

I was so refreshed to read just today of the journey of Sharon and Hugo Anson, who were childless for twelve years. Their primary battle was with cliché-wielding Christians – but their faith shines with hope mingled with reality.

> People would occasionally prophesy over us, telling us we would have a child. It felt like all the pain people had experienced through once being childless came out on us. I found that very abusive. People would say the reason we were not having children was because of pride or because we were more interested in our ministry than in having a family. Part of me wanted to tell them the medical facts, but another part didn't bother trying to explain...[4]

Thank God for the Normans of the world. We need people with some prayer muscle to help some of us six stone

---

[4] *Christianity and Renewal*, January 2002

weaklings to move beyond being completely ineffective, like skinny nerds on a beach having the sand kicked in our faces by Satan on a daily basis. But don't measure yourself against their stories and successes: they are true all right – most of them. But they are not the whole truth.

I'm so thankful for the almost brutal honesty of the New Testament. Paul the apostle is never presented as a swashbuckling super-hero, despite his huge achievements. He writes to the contentious Corinthians and lets them know of his weariness and depression – feeling as one 'who is under sentence of death.'[5] And there is no plastic portrait of a unrealistically confident Jesus skipping and jumping towards Golgotha daubed in the pages of Scripture: he kneels beneath gargantuan, back-breaking agony; he is overwhelmed by the sorrow and pain that is about to break over him like a huge, bloody dam.

Jesus is the Victor – and victory requires battle. Battle is not a precise, antiseptic science, but the ebb and flow of breakthrough and wounding, of the adrenaline rush that comes from winning and the bone-numbing weariness that comes from marching just one more mile. All of this was true of Jesus: and it's true of Norman too.

The past doesn't determine the future

Remember that rabid, intoxicating enthusiasm that you felt when you became a Christian? For me, it was the most breathtaking, exhilarating time of my life. I was so desperate to let people know that I had found God that I am sure that I probably was totally off-putting to most. I had a Jesus badge the size of a dustbin lid on my lapel,

---

[5] 2 Corinthians 1:9

and there were so many plastic fishes plastered across the back of my car that it resembled a mobile aquarium. Subtlety was not a consideration: my badge screamed a gentle message like *HELLO, YOU'RE GOING TO HELL!* or *WILL YOU MISS THE ABYSS?*

My early attempts at sharing my faith consisted of a literally breathless monologue where I would misquote a lengthy string of scriptures. But while I was short on biblical accuracy, I was loaded with enthusiasm. Why the wondrous thrill? Well, part of it was the joy of discovery. The Bible was like a sparkling treasure chest brimming over with priceless gems of truth; I couldn't understand most if it, and couldn't tell the difference between the Old Testament, the New Testament, and the maps at the back, but the thrill of being on this brand new spiritual safari was intoxicating. But another source of the bubbling joy was the sheer luxury of being able to look at the future with hope; what I had been in the past was not going to dictate the future of me any more; why, I was a brand spanking new creation in Christ – now, everything was possible. I was filled with hope; a delightful springtime season of change was in the air.

A distant cousin of this hope for change can be found every New Year's Eve: thousands throng the streets for the big countdown to midnight, and while for some it is little more than another reason to get into an alcohol-induced haze, for many the birth of a new year signals the possibility that life might yet be different. The chimes of Big Ben signal, we hope and pray, the advent of a yet unstained year, for at least a second or two. Perhaps the world will be more peaceful; perhaps we, with our resolutions, might be a little more loving, healthy, rich, content, thin, or successful. For many brand new Christians, hope for change is a major source of joy. Why, they are going to be altered – and they believe that they will alter their world as a result.

But then new Christians settle down. Sometimes they land with a huge bump, shot out of the sky by the lack of hope and joy exhibited by Christians who have been around for a while. The Bible becomes something you read because that's what Christians do, isn't it? The voyage of discovery descends into a sad, tedious maintenance programme. And one of the most tragic casualties of this settling is the death of hope. We give up believing that we can change the world – or indeed that we ourselves can be changed. Stuck in a groove, we peer at the future through the sad eyes of those who are condemned to be forever the same. A leopard can't change its spots, we insist. And as we settle into that shadowy land, we are prey to all kinds of temptations. Hope, however, is the moral force that acts a crash barrier that bounces me back from the cliff side when I would rather throw myself headfirst into the temporary insanity that is sin. Hope is the engine that keeps us walking forward to another day, believing that we can yet be transformed, albeit slowly and painfully, into a being a better, stronger person than we are now.

But the hiss from hell tells me that I will never be better or stronger than I am; that holiness is a doctrine that I fear but could never be a reality that I could actually experience; thus I am crushed into believing that I might just as well get on with being who I am, and sin away. My failure and judgment is inevitable anyway, so what's the point of any attempt towards moral heroism? I am doomed to be as I am – or so I am deluded into thinking.

Peter, the once hopeful fisherman, was mugged by hopelessness. Even after three breathtaking years in the company of Jesus, Peter sulked and descended into a deep despair. His problems were not generated by a suicidal angst with the world, but with a terminally hopeless gaze into the inner world of Peter himself. But a brief breakfast with Jesus changed all of that. Peter was not destined to go down in history as the terminal failure with 'denial' tattooed on his forehead, but as the fearless apostle, the one from whose shadows power and healing throbbed. A thousand resurrections are possible. What has been does not have to be in the future: you and I can change. We are followers of the One who transforms.

Prayer is learned

Some actions in life come naturally to healthy human beings – like bowel movements, breathing, and blinking: they are some of the fundamental mechanisms of physical existence. But most of the basic actions of bodily co-ordination are the result of learning and practice. Moving the limbs is an unlearned reflex: but co-ordinating that movement into the effortless grace that is walking requires a lot of training and practice – and not a few heavy crash landings on one's backside in the process.

We can labour under the impression that prayer is simply doing what comes naturally. After all, we love Jesus, don't we – so therefore prayer *ought* to be easier than it is. Really? Just how natural is it to have what is occasionally (let's get real – most of the time) a one-sided conversation – with someone that you can't see? The truth is that *all* communication is the result of a journey of learning, be it in the development of vocabulary and expression, in the understanding of body language and how it relates to our communication, or in the understanding of the more subtle arts of tact, diplomacy and timing.

Prayer is not as easy as breathing, but is the fruit of committed apprenticeship. Thus the disciples asked Jesus to teach them how to pray. And so Paul encourages Timothy to 'train himself' in godliness – the word used there is *gumnaze* – the root for our gymnasium.[6]

As a card-carrying member of the local gym who has demonstrated my commitment to regular gym attendance by the payment of high annual fees – and actually showing up there twice in the last two years – I can testify to the fact that, most of the time, I don't really feel like donning my yellow leotard and heading to the torture chamber. Gyms aren't made for people who always feel like working out (although I understand that exercise can be addictive – a life-controlling force that I've never personally struggled with). Rather, the gym requires perseverance, energy and a refusal to give up even though you're surrounded by muscle-bound 'gods' who apparently bench press large trucks. Running a marathon isn't easy. Lifting heavy weights takes practice. And prayer is a skill we need to grow in: not one that we're born with.

Something old, something new, something borrowed...

Sometimes we think that we're bad at praying, whereas actually it's our methods and approaches to prayer that have become tedious and worn out. We're not bad, just bored. I've said it now, and don't throw those stones at me, please. Let's face it: the practice of prayer can be boring. It isn't easy settling yourself down for a warm conversation with an invisible Friend. It's wonderful

---

[6] 1 Timothy 4:7

when we can approach these encounters with faith and expectancy, but there are times when prayer seems like a ridiculous exercise of talking with One who doesn't appear to respond (at least not in the immediate conversational sense). Prayer is sometimes exhilarating, and sometimes a bit like having a good chat with the ceiling. Are our words even penetrating through the plaster up there?

I've discovered that we can grow in prayer as we use different approaches to prayer. For some time, since a friendly bishop introduced me to it, I've been using the Anglican prayer book as a basis for my prayers, sometimes first thing in the morning, and sometimes in the closing moments before sleep. It's taken me a while to get used to opening a prayer book...

First of all, I had problems with knowing where I was in the seasons of the so-called Christian year. I knew about Advent (all those cardboard calendars with little doors you open and Mars Bars to scoff) but beyond that, I was all at sea when it came to Epiphanies and high days and holidays; I thought that Michaelmas had something to do with Marks & Spencer's. And then the very idea of what seemed like sanctified script reading from an ancient and modern autocue didn't seem appealing to a spontaneity-obsessed non-conformist type like me. But I pressed through, and, in encountering the power of liturgy, I made the simple discovery that I don't pray more than I do *because I simply can't think of anything useful to say*. To take the carefully shaped words of another, words that are the fruit of meditation and reflection and therefore leap and dance with biblical truth, words that have been the comfort of believers through the centuries, has added another dimension to my spirituality.

So what's going on? Am I becoming an undercover Anglican? No, I'm just discovering the thrill of approaching my spirituality in a different way. To insist that we always pray the same way is as tedious as eating the same meal over and over, or insisting that love-making always follows the precise same pattern. This is a predictability that makes the divine dull. And the impression of the formation of dullness around the person of God is a scandal.

Annie Dillard laments

> Week after week I was moved by the pitiableness of the bare linoleum floored sacristy which no flowers could cheer or soften, by the terrible singing I so loved, by the fatigued Bible readings, the lagging emptiness and dilution of the liturgy, the horrifying vacuity of the sermon, and by the fog of senselessness pervading the whole, which existed along-side, and probably caused, the wonder of the fact that we came; we returned; we showed up; week after week we went through with it...[7]

Perhaps your prayer life is in the doldrums. Why not sit down for a few minutes and ask whether it's not that *prayer* is boring – perhaps *you* are! Do you always kneel to pray? Then go for a walk. Is your praying of the loud, aggressive *'God isn't deaf but he isn't nervous either, so there'* kind? Then give your mouth a well-earned vacation and try the sound of silence. Do you consider icons and images to be the stamping ground of sincerely misled idolaters? Well, lighten up, literally. Break out a candle and let its flickering flame warm your soul. Do something different, for God's sake.

You can pray. And you can grow in prayer.

---

[7] Annie Dillard, *Teaching a Stone to Talk* (HarperCollins, 1982)

2

Tell yourself that the only good prayers are long prayers...

'When you pray, say...'

> *'Pray as you can, and not as you can't'*
> – *Dom Chapman*

The heaters were ancient, ugly contraptions that hung down from the ceilings of the tin-roofed mission church. Switched on and off by a long chain, they hissed and crackled during our services, and produced comfort and torture in turn. Their smell was the welcome scent of the familiar, like dusty books in libraries or roast potatoes on Sundays. The smell of them spoke to us, announcing the glad news that we were together again for our weekly celebration, when we stepped out of our swirling mist worlds and gathered to peer at a vision that was clear and sharply focused, through the fogs into the core of certainty that we felt sure was at the heart of it all. Pensioners forgot their bills and aches and pains, youngsters laid aside their fear of spots and being uncool, and we tiptoed into the presence of God with our loud songs and our hopeful hands raised skyward.

Let the fire fall, let the fire fall, let the fire from heaven fall!
We are waiting, and expecting, now in faith dear Lord we
    call
Let the fire fall, let the fire fall, on Thy promise we depend
With the Holy Ghost from heaven let the Pentecostal fire
    descend

Sometimes it seemed that the fire had indeed fallen on someone: their shortened breathing would let us know that they were more excited and animated than the rest of us. Their enthusiasm bubbled over, erupted even, as they swayed and clapped and spoke in the strange language we called *tongues*. But most of the time it was the heaters that at first warmed our backs and then slow-roasted us into a vague sleepiness...

But although there were the tiresome times, those prayer meetings were also filled with very beautiful moments, when it seemed that God was walking around the place, hugs and smiles scattered everywhere as he did.

Three decades later, I can still hear the poetry of their prayers as if it were yesterday. Many of them were rough and ready EastEnders who felt that God should be addressed in a posher voice than their own. Like my own, their natural speech was a little short on 'h' sounds. 'Ow are yer mate? Orrible weather, don't yer fink?' is perhaps a slight exaggeration, but Henry Higgins would have had a nightmare with our church, for whom the rain in Spain did not fall gently on the plain, if you get my drift. I remember that with huge fondness and great appreciation: what wonderful friends of God – and to me – they were.

Our prayers must have sounded like the mock pompous voice of a haughty butler: 'Great and gracious hah-heavenly Father, we come into thy presence today in

the most mighty and, hem, majestic name of Jesus...'
Some of us pronounced the Lord's name as *Yay-zuss*,
which implied that we were fluent in Hebrew or at least
had been to Israel for our holidays...

They weren't being pretentious, just respectful. Of
course, God wanted to hear them just as they were: no
elocution lessons were required. But I remember the lilting rise and fall of their voices as they poured out their
hearts to God at great length. They would quote reams
of Scripture with fluent ease. Some might quietly weep;
this was no emotionalism but the fruit of their genuine
love for the Lord Jesus. Many of these folks had been
dealt a difficult hand in life, but theirs was a simple trust
in God. Their love for Jesus drew me like a moth to light;
but I just couldn't ever aspire to their praying technique.
And they never demanded that I did. I would sometimes
stand to my feet during the prayer meeting, and pray
loudly the most absurd and ridiculous tosh. Next to our
church building there stood a bus stop, which gave me a
lovely opportunity to pray, with great gusto, that God
would 'Save all those people on the bus, Lord. Fill 'em
with the Holy Ghost! Heal any sick people on the bus!
Raise the dead on the bus!!' Bus travel among the dead is
rare: the possibility of physical resurrection on board a
London Transport vehicle is unlikely. But those prayer
'warriors', as we used to call them, refused to allow me
to be intimidated by my lack of thoughtfulness; they
inspired but never crushed new Christians.

I can't pray like that...

I think that the disciples of Jesus probably felt intimidated by others who were apparently better at prayer than
they were. Perhaps they shifted uncomfortably in their

half sleep on those days when Jesus stirred himself in the crisp cold of the dawning hours and wandered off to confer with his Father about the coming day. Did they feel some pang of guilt as they turned over and huddled back down in the welcome warmth of their cloaks to catch some more sleep? None of the disciples came from a background of practised spirituality – they were amateurs at prayer, and asked their Master to teach them how to do it.[1]

I imagine that they would have been intimidated by the eloquence and dress-to-impress piety of the Pharisees, as they prayed at volume on the street corners. These trained experts in public prayer were required to pray for a minimum of three hours each day; their Rolls Royce silver-tongued petitions would have made the friends of Jesus shrink as they ambled by in their little Robin Reliants of prayer.

The rabbis were convinced that the only good praying was long praying – Jesus links their wide open mouths with their inflated egos: 'The teachers of the law for a show make lengthy prayers.'[2] In the evangelical subculture, a similar idea still exists today, even if only at a subconscious level. If you're going to pray, it had better be for at least an hour. And while it *is* good to set quality time aside to spend with God, the bitter irony is that often, because we feel that we can't pray for an hour, we don't pray at all, and we miss the golden opportunity for 'mini-Sabbaths'. Isn't it better to *pray* for five minutes than to *aspire to pray* for an hour; and indeed, to believe passionately that hour long praying is the way to go but not pray at all? If we have this 'never mind the quality, feel the width' approach to prayer, then we miss out on the opportunity of just being with Jesus.

---

[1] Luke 11:1
[2] Mark 12:40

Prayer as technique

In some senses, prayer is a technique, an art, a skill, in the same way that all communication is a learned skill – we established that in the last chapter. But we can become obsessed with the mechanism of communication rather than the person with whom we are communicating. Richard Foster points out that we are in a danger zone whenever we become preoccupied with spiritual discipline in and of itself, rather than preoccupied with the God with whom we meet through the disciplines.

> It is a pitfall to view the disciplines as virtuous in themselves. In and of themselves, the disciplines have no virtue, possess no righteousness, contain no rectitude. It was this important truth that the Pharisees failed to see. The disciplines place us before God; they do not give us Brownie points with God.[3]

Women are sometimes heard to complain that men are often more preoccupied with sexual technique than lovemaking. These men view the distant orgasm as the ultimate tape to be breasted at the conclusion of an epic performance. In a spirit of competitiveness and macho pride, they insist that only a medal-winning display is good enough; whereas their partner wants real closeness and warmth – and not necessarily an award-winning encounter. Sex like this is reduced to athletically inspirational coupling rather than real lovemaking – and the person with whom we engage in sex is not so much a partner, but more an apparatus, available for the slaking of a testosterone-fed thirst. In some cases, once the performance is

---

[3] Richard Foster, *Prayer: Finding the Heart's True Home* (London: Hodder & Stoughton, 1992)

over, then, tragically, the human 'apparatus' can be discarded. And an unhealthy preoccupation with technique can develop even in the security of the strongest marriages.

In just the same way, there's a danger that we can almost worship prayer itself, as if the pursuit of prayer as a habit carries its own rewards. We are thus engaging in spirituality, but a self-directed spirituality which does not cause us to bump into God, but merely allows us to feel we have done our duty.. The task has been completed, the check list ticked – but we have still not engaged with God. Similar things happen in worship: the practice of 'worshipping worship' is very common today. I am delighted and encouraged at the plethora of worship conferences, well-composed songs and the variety of excellently produced CDs that worship music fans can enjoy. But it worries me when sung worship becomes the big experience that we must all have every time we get together, as if the enjoyment of what can be little more than a well-constructed community sing song is inherently meritorious. I don't want to be purist about it, and often find myself enjoying the crowd dynamic or the excellent musicianship that can be found in large worship gatherings, just for their own sake. But worship ultimately is not a consumer item to be picked over like the last release from *Pop Idol*: it is the means by which we can serenade God and exhort one another – and therefore it is a means to an end, and not the end itself. And there are times when we feel no desire whatsoever to pray or worship – and that's when healthy, disciplined choices must be made.

Prayer as discipline

While *technique* should not be our priority, we will nevertheless need to embrace discipline if we are to pray at all. But 'discipline' is not a popular word these days. It conjures up images of wide-eyed, staring fanatics from the past – and there have been a few, who can't be faulted for their commitment, but may have been a bit short-changed when wisdom was being handed out – saints who lived for years on pillars, or never washed. The follies and excesses of medieval ascetics led many of the reformers to reject the idea of disciplined spirituality – particular those who had come from such a background. Martin Luther despised the concept of spiritual disciplines, believing that he would ultimately have killed himself if he had continued his slavish commitment to prayers, vigils, reading, fasting and other exercises of discipline.

Some would try to argue that Isaiah and the Lord himself spoke against practices like fasting and rituals of worship.[4] In reality both were not speaking out against the *habit* of fasting, but rather the *abuse* of the disciplines. So fasting in an attempt to manipulate God, or impress others, is wrong. But Jesus was not writing off the disciplines; rather he was seeking to protect their integrity. Put most simply, your prayer life – and mine – will only be what we choose it to be. Maturity in prayer will not mug us in our sleep, blossom as the result of our being in some 'special' meeting or service, or grow in any way without our making conscious, realistic and specific choices on a daily basis. There's no shortcut behind our will.

Psychiatrist M. Scott Peck observes

There are many people I know who possess a vision of personal evolution yet seem to lack the will for it. They want, and believe it is possible, to skip over the discipline, to find an easy shortcut to sainthood. Often they attempt to attain

---

[4] Isaiah 58, 59; Matthew 23

it by simply imitating the superficialities of saints, retiring to the desert or taking up carpentry. Some even believe that by such imitation they have really become saints and prophets, and are unable to acknowledge that they are still children and face the painful fact that they must start at the beginning and go through the middle.[5]

And so, while we don't want to get enslaved in legalistic asceticism, we must face the fact that choice, will, and discipline are essential ingredients if we are to move further down the pathway of prayer.

Stephen Travis laments our lack in this area

In the modern church, qualities such as perseverance and loyalty are in short supply. In an age of instant coffee, instant glue and instant bank loans, we don't take easily to the pain of sticking to unglamorous tasks, or developing a discipline in prayer. But as Samuel Chadwick said, 'All God's things are grown things. He is never in the ready-made business.' [6]

For me, the choices begin at the start of each day when I am doing my 'Lazarus lookalike – before Jesus came by' impersonation in the shower. Feeling like a drenched corpse, and drifting into the required level of consciousness needed in order to negotiate yet another full day of existence on planet Earth, I have to decide: will I begin this day by rushing to the computer to hear that joyfully irritating 'You've got mail' voice – or will I climb onto my exercise bike and pick up my Bible and prayer book as I pedal my way to nowhere? Of course, the former takes no effort at all. Discipline is my bridge to a tended, manicured, cared-for life.

---

[5] M. Scott Peck, *The Road Less Travelled* (Arrow, 1990)

[6] Stephen Travis, *You've Got Mail* (Carlisle: Spring Harvest/Authentic, 2002)

Passion and simplicity

Richard Foster, that masterful writer on prayer and discipline, was a big shock to me when I met him personally. I had expected a measured, serious sage, a modern day saint of few words and fewer smiles. He is the opposite: Foster is a man who is deeply in love with God, and who exudes a sense of fun, relaxation and occasional hilarity. He writes movingly about the simplicity of prayer

> We may have been taught that prayer is a sublime and other worldly activity; that in prayer we are to talk to God about God. As a result we are inclined to view our experiences as distractions and intrusions into proper prayer. This is an ethereal, decarnate spirituality. We, on the other hand, worship a God who was born in a smelly stable, who walked this earth in blood, sweat, and tears, but who nevertheless lived in perpetual responsiveness to the heavenly Monitor. And so I urge you: carry on an ongoing conversation with God about the daily stuff of life, a little like Tevye in *Fiddler on the Roof*. For now, do not worry about 'proper' praying, just talk to God. Share your hurts; share your sorrows; share your joys – freely and openly. God listens in compassion and love, just as we do when our children come to us. He delights in our presence...[7]

I'm nervous about the complicating of spirituality. Michael Eaton says, 'Jesus asks for simplicity in prayer rather than verbosity or complexity.' As Rob Warner says, 'there are times when the simple cry of "Father" sums up all that needs to be said in prayer.'

---

[7] Richard Foster, *Prayer: Finding the Heart's True Home* (London: Hodder & Stoughton, 1992).

I have sat through too many occasions of public prayer when I couldn't help wondering who was actually being addressed. Was this finely manicured speech I could hear intended for heaven's ear, or was it a work of oratory designed to impress more carnal, human ears? That's not to say that a public prayer can't be a stirring tapestry of oratory, peppered with biblical truth. But when we take that as our model for private prayer, we end up with a relationship based on speeches: hardly a recipe for intimacy. The Lord's Prayer is profound in its simplicity: we do well to emulate it.

Moment by moment...

Walking through shared experiences develops intimacy. That's one reason why I don't do very well when I'm alone. No matter how beautiful the sunset, it pales if I cannot celebrate its splendour with somebody. Over the last couple of decades Kay and I have spent many holidays with Chris and Jeanne Edwardson, friends from Oregon. One of the many reasons that we love spending time together is their practice of celebrating and being grateful for the fun that we're having together: our conversations are peppered with 'Isn't this great? It doesn't get much better than this, does it?'

Shared experiences aren't limited to those special sunset moments: the chatter of everyday life can be like a building block of human relationships. Friendships that demand that no 'small' talk be permitted, and that sharing can only be centred around the important, the significant, and the sublime, wear me out. Sometimes we all want to talk small stuff! I believe that the same is true in prayer. We need to learn to chatter with God, who apparently is never bored by our 'prattle'.

To return to the marriage analogy, (and if it seems that I do, a lot, in this book, it's because I think that there are many parallels between the intimacy of prayer and that of communication and sexuality within marriage), no woman wants a man who only wants to talk at a specific hour of the evening when sex is on the agenda: she looks for a developed, consistent sharing that doesn't just kick in when hormones signal that time again. Trying to talk to God in the thirty minute slot so especially prescribed, without any ongoing conversation during the day, will produce a stilted, awkward praying. I say again: chatter on. He loves it.

Realistic goals in prayer

As we come to the end of this chapter, I want to encourage you to make some goals that are realistic and achievable in your relationship with God. If you're anything like me, you pop off to some prayer conference and the result is that you pledge to pray for countless hours every day, arising at some impossible time in the morning. Of course, it doesn't happen, but we feel that anything less than a huge commitment is, well, so unworthy.

I hinted about this earlier in the chapter, but let's return to this little discussion on this odd practice of *fantasy commitment*. We feel that to determine to pray for two hours seems appropriate – far more so than a determination to set aside five minutes of quietness and reflection. We thus enter a land of noble aspirations – that result in nothing. Consider this – isn't it better to actually spend five minutes with God, than to believe in the furtive idea of spending two hours with him – but actually, in reality the result is that you spend no time at all? Realised objectives are better than noble myths. And

it's not only in the realm of prayer that fantasy commitment manifests itself. I could take you to churches
where Christians go forward to offer themselves as
missionaries to far flung places in the world, but if you
asked them to move from the pew that they occupy
every Sunday to another part of the building, or to tell
the chap who lives next door about Jesus, there would be
a rebellion. It's easier to believe that I would win thousands to Christ were I to be a missionary than it is to
invite the family next door over for dinner. Thus our
commitment remains in the fantasyland of our minds. So
go ahead – get radical. Make a five minute appointment
with God sometime during today. It could well be the
first step towards praying as you can – and not praying
as you can't.

3

Try and just go it alone

'Say, *Our* Father...'

> *'What is life if we have not life together?'*
> *– T.S. Eliot*

When Jesus taught his friends to pray *'Our'* Father, he confronted the myth that solitary prayer is the only or best way to pray, and that we somehow don't need the mutuality and strength that comes from being part of a community of prayer – the church. Put most simply, prayer with friends is usually easier. Ishmael, the Duracell-powered children's minister, is my occasional prayer partner. This requires me to do a lot of bouncing, but is very beneficial. It's a relief to surrender to the truth that, when it comes to spirituality, we really do need each other – we need church; this is by design. But I am nervous, lest we shrink the church down to being merely a support group for little us. Some treat the church with a consumer attitude that reduces it to being nothing more than a feeding centre designed to keep them warm. When the service – literally – is not to their liking or taste, they move on, the 'Lord having told them to leave.' Such an attitude dwarfs and minimises the church. Let's pan the camera out to a wider screen view for a few moments, to see that the praying church is more than a blessing club; it is God's gift to a lonely planet. The invitation to come in from the cold, in a culture of arctic techno-isolation, is God's loving call for shivering humanity. But the fireside will only be warm in the church that knows how to engage with God in worship and prayer.

We must reaffirm the value of church, lest we, in our culture that is obsessed with the personal (personal Walkman, personal trainer, personal pizza, personal Jesus), end up with no coherent doctrine or understanding of the church at all. Church can rankle: she irritates us, slows us down, winds us up, and seems to defy even the costliest and most energy-sapping attempts to make her more effective. Billions of pounds are invested in her annually, but in some parts of the world she is shrinking, despite all of the cash injection. If she were a corporation, her end of year results would mean that they'd fire the managing director. At times she seems more like a withered, ugly crone than a blushing bride. We look back with pride at some of her historic exploits: slaves freed, nations reached, freedoms won, the oppressed brought in from the cold. But we peer over our shoulders and weep with shame too: the screams reverberate from the inquisitor's rack; we blush at the harassment of Galileo because he insisted that the world was round. We lower our heads at the political shenanigans and power struggles, the blood-letting of the Crusades by warriors with signs of the cross on their chests. The church has a chequered history.

But she is still one of God's finest ideas – perhaps that in itself, while not excusing her, helps us to understand why she has so often been the object of satanic hijacking throughout history. She is the appointed one, ordained to yell back an answer to the orphan culture that is every generation: 'You are loved! You are loved.' And never was there a time when the gentle, yet firm voice of a praying, Jesus-centred church was more needed.

Our culture is suffering from techno-isolation: we have ever more efficient methods of hyper-fast communication, and yet with all of our gadgets and gizmos, we still long for more than a computerised voice that announces we've got mail. We want the warmth and spontaneity of real, face-to-face conversation, we are hungry for community and friendship. Rapid change, household fragmentation, and increased mobility are contributing factors to loneliness being the epidemic of the third millennium. For some, the most time-consuming intimate relationship they have is with a computer chip. But try as we might, we still need relationship and community.

The most popular 'soaps' on television are all centred on the dynamics of life, sometimes very mundane life in community. Consider the huge popularity of *EastEnders*, *Coronation Street*, *Neighbours*, *Home and Away*, and more... their characters are often adulterous and sometimes murderous scoundrels, and yet they are people *together*. Be it in the Rovers Return, the Queen Vic, or in an Australian suburb where a 'neighbour is just a footstep away', these people gravitate around a centrality that is community. The Americans have their own versions in the hugely popular *Friends* and the now defunct *Cheers*. The opening lyrics from that bar-centred comedy say it all

Sometimes you wanna go where everybody knows your
name
And they're always glad you came
You wanna be where you can see
Troubles are all the same
You wanna go where everyone knows your name.

And now, if all those soaps were not enough, we have the television smash hit of the early third millennium: reality television. Who would have thought that *Big Brother* would stand a chance of success? Stick a group of ordinary people in a camera-riddled house for weeks on end, film their every waking and sleeping moment; give them unexciting and mundane tasks to do. I wonder how well that proposal was first received when it surfaced in a television boardroom. Millions have been hooked.

The docu-soap provides us with helpful insights concerning the daily experiences of an airport cleaner, who is doing a very valuable job – but who would have ever thought it to be the stuff of television? Extreme reality shows like *Survivor* give us the chance to see what happens in relationships under extreme conditions. Internet chat forums provide opportunity for interaction and relationship – but getting information from the information super highway is not enough. We still need to rub shoulders; half a million different types of support groups (such as Alcoholics Anonymous) exist in the USA, evidence of our need for authentic close encounters.

What does all this scream at us? The missing ingredient in third millennium Britain is relationships. And when the church takes notice of this, she wins.

The phenomenal impact of Alpha, (in excess of a million now have completed the course in the UK), which is a relational, interactive method of exploring the claims of Christ, testifies to this truth. But think again about Alpha: it is more than a yuppie supper club with a dose of God stuff sprinkled on the dessert; more than a series of lectures with food. With its insistence on emphasising encounters with God through the Holy Spirit, Alpha has at its heart a call to intimacy with God, love discovered not only through information but through encounter with the Living Lover. Our culture is more than lonely and techno-isolated: it is estranged from God. Britain needs more than social club churches; the urgent call is for fun, dynamic, human, relevant, *spiritual* communities that gather together around God. Churches that are, as Dallas Willard says, 'communities of prayerful love'.

Donald Baillie provides a memorable image of what has gone wrong in our culture, in his insistence that the plan of redemption is the great 'tale of God calling his human children to form a great circle for the playing of his game'

> In that circle we ought all to be standing, linked together with lovingly joined hands, facing towards the Light in the centre, which is God ('the Love that moves the sun and the other stars'); seeing our fellow creatures all round the circle in the light of that central Love, which shines on them and beautifies their faces; and joining with them in the dance of God's great game, the rhythm of love universal. But instead of that, we have, each one, turned our backs upon God and the circle of our fellows, and faced the other way, so that we can see neither the Light at the centre nor the faces on the circumference. And indeed in that position it is difficult even to join hands with our fellows! Therefore instead of playing God's game we play, each one, our own selfish little game... Each one of us wishes to be the centre, and there is blind confusion, and not even any true knowledge of God or of our neighbours. That is what is wrong...[1]

I remember with gratitude the day that I first bumped into a small band of people who were playing God's game.

---

[1] Donald Baillie, quoted in *You've Got Mail*, the Spring Harvest Study Guide, 2002

Happy day

To be blunt, they were quite an odd-looking group, or so I thought.

They sat in a circle, on a mixture of threadbare armchairs and even older settees that had been thoughtfully 'donated' to the church. The room where they sat was called 'the Minor Hall'. Not that there was a *major* hall; but this room was reserved for after-church cups of tea, plates of biscuits, and – on this occasion – the Sunday night 'afterglow'. This strangely named event was not, as I feared, a time of ritually sacrificing the old ladies, ('Come on then lads, let's chuck Sister Doris on the fire, she'll burn...') but rather an informal time of sipping PG Tips, singing, and telling each other about what God had been up to in the previous week. Looking back, it was all rather wonderful, but this was my first time in the church, and I was nervous, slightly terrified even. I scanned their faces anxiously. Some had their eyes glued shut, their features a mask of worshipful concentration, their hands held aloft. I understood the shut-eyed approach, but why did they stick their hands up in the air? Were they asking to be excused to use the toilet – one hand if you'd quite like to go, two hands up if you're pretty well desperate? I pondered the meaning of their charismatic devotion. Others sat back in their tatty chairs, relaxed, eyes opened, no intensity for them, just enjoying the atmosphere of togetherness. A guitarist strummed a few chords, and I noticed that he didn't seem to be performing for anyone: he didn't look round to the group for approval of his playing; in fact, he moved through the chord changes with his eyes closed too.

Even the song was odd.

Great is the Lord, and greatly to be praised
In the city of our God, in the mountain of His holiness
Beautiful for situation, the joy of the whole earth
Is Mount Zion on the side of the north the city of the great
   King?

Yikes! What lyrics were these? 'Beautiful for situation' seemed an odd way of saying that a location was nice. Imagine the sales blurb in the estate agent's window: 'Three bedroom house, new bathroom, power shower, large back garden, in all beautiful for situation....'

And what in the name of reason was all that 'Is Mount Zion on the side of the north?' stuff? Were they asking for directions? If so, why sing the request to each other? It was, as Alice would say, 'Curiouser and curiouser...'

I watched them, standing by the door, too afraid to join their circle, but strangely aware that they had something that was way beyond my grasp.

The song ended, and the kettle had come to the boil, and so 'the time of fellowship' began. I couldn't escape now – and anyway, I realised with some alarm, I didn't want to. One after another, without making me some kind of embarrassed centre of attention, they came and shook my hand and smiled and murmured that they were glad that I was there, and the weirdest thing of all – I knew that they really were glad. When they asked me what I had thought about the earlier evening service, I didn't feel interrogated. They all knew that I wasn't a Christian, but nobody selected me for a good gospel thrashing. No one attempted to ram anything down my throat; they seemed real, honest – and they were rather big on God. Within an hour I found myself quietly kneeling to begin the nearly thirty-year-old journey as a Christian that continues today. And then they formed a long line – literally – that went all the way to the back of the building as they delightedly welcomed me into the family of God.

I had found a loving church – and I will always be in their debt. In the coming months those people listened to my ridiculous questions – but never made me feel small. They didn't tut-tut when I used the contents page of my Bible, even though they could flip right to the portion of Scripture with precision and ease. Carless, they gave me lifts to and from church, even when it was very late. They took me out for pizza and treated me as if I were a lifelong friend. And when they sensed that I was messing up in my personal behaviour, they didn't lecture or scold or give me a haughty glare, but gently, kindly guided me as I allowed them to. Yes, I had found a loving church. Looking back, the songs that we sung were pretty cheesy. I'm not even sure about some of the legalistic taboos that were the common currency of our little church community. Not everything was right, and with church it never is.

But I fell in love with God because of them, and I began a romance with his church as well. I'm uncomfortable around the cynics who seem to love to celebrate the weaknesses of the church. For me, it was and is a community that welcomed me in from the cold; that church spoke hope and life into my troubled young heart, and became a genuine family to me. God is head over heels in love with the church; certainly, it's flawed: but it can be very, very beautiful. Thirty years ago, I got a firsthand taste of its glory.

I hadn't been back to that rusty old tin building for years, but, passing through the town, I decided to stop by on the off chance that someone might be in there. I knocked on the door, and the young man, turned older, who had strummed that guitar so many years earlier opened it. Initially he didn't recognise me – time has not been that kind in my case – but once I introduced myself, I was greeted once again with a big, wide smile and open arms.

I wandered back into 'the Minor Hall'. The old chairs were long gone – and many of the people who had sat in them on that long lost night of my youth were no longer to be seen. But it felt like a holy moment as I stood quietly, alone for a while, and remembered their songs, their kindness, and their love.

I'll always be grateful that I bumped into a loving church. Grateful forever. Literally.

Prayer at the heart of the game

What was it about those people that was so magnetic and inviting? As I said, they were certainly kind and welcoming, but there was a special, deeper something about them. I am convinced that I was compelled by their sense of devotion to Jesus. They seemed to be good people, but there was more than sterile purity and cold morality. They enjoyed one another's company, but they were more than a good club to join. And as for their style – frankly, it was alien to me. But I found them compelling because they were a diverse group of people who shared a common love; their spirituality was arresting and real. I had caught a whiff of what Keith Miller calls 'the scent of love'. It was an intoxicating, heady fragrance.

The early church grew not because of the spiritual gifts of Christians such as the gift of speaking in tongues and not because Christianity was such a palatable doctrine (to the contrary; it is about the most unpalatable doctrine there is) but because they had discovered the secret of community.

Generally they did not have to lift a finger to evangelise. Someone would be walking down a back alley in Corinth or Ephesus and would see a group of people sitting together talking about the strangest things – something about a man and a tree and an execution and an empty tomb. What they were talking about made no sense to the onlooker. But there was something about the way they spoke to one another, about the way they looked at one another, about the way they cried together, the way they laughed together, the way they touched one another that was strangely appealing. It gave off the scent of love. The onlooker would start to drift farther down the alley; only to be pulled back to this little group like a bee to a flower. He would listen some more, still not understanding, and start to drift away again. But again he would be pulled back, thinking, I don't have the slightest idea what these people are talking about, but whatever it is, I want part of it.[2]

I certainly wanted a part of it that night. Three decades later, I still do. And I am convinced that the greatest need in the world today is for a church that is at ease with prayer, but also at ease with each other. Nothing else will really do. The church that has not learned to be together with Jesus in the place of prayer may be adept at changing the social conditions of its community for the better. But if spirituality is not at the heart of social action, it is diluted into a vague do-goodism that leads to little more than liberal evangelicalism. For sure, people's lives are made better: but the *reason* for the improvement lies beyond their grasp; they fail to see that it is because of the love of God that life has improved. Their eternity remains unchanged and untouched. Their environment might be better, but their hearts remain unmoved and unreached.

---

[2] Keith Miller, *The Scent of Love* (Smithmark, 1983)

The church that does not centre itself in prayer will turn passionate evangelism into cold expansionism at best (church growth for its own sake) and, at worst, will stop sharing the good news with clarity and passion altogether. Distance from the heartbeat of God will cause a gradual erosion of enthusiasm for mission. At first the shift will be slow and almost imperceptible. Only after a few years will some pause, look back, and ask the haunting question: 'Whatever happened to mission and evangelism? Why do we no longer know the joy and mess of having brand new Christians around?' And new Christians are the lifeblood, the *raison d'être* for the church's very existence.

The church that does not centre its action and activities around prayer will eventually be driven more by market forces and consumer demands than the heart and intentions of God. Its services and meetings may dispense good, orthodox information *about* God: and yet there will be few opportunities for the theory to become reality. Indeed, many churches become little more than carefully designed mechanisms that are actually constructed to keep God at a healthy distance, where a theology of the imminence of God is part of their orthodoxy, but the suggestion that God might actually do anything other than speak through the pages of the preached Bible are met with corporately raised eyebrows of deep suspicion.

We must learn and hold on to the joy of whispering and shouting, 'Our Father' together. The disciplines of silence and solitude are being rediscovered as we search for a coherent evangelical spirituality: but let's not emphasise them at the expense of community devotion. As Michael Moynagh writes

In the past standardised congregations required everyone to sit, stand and kneel at the same time. They were instructed what to think through the sermon, and it was expected that they would all believe roughly the same. People who did not fit the mould left. The evacuation of the church since the 1950s involved a flight from this uniform approach.

Some people have taken refuge in highly individualistic forms of spirituality, spirituality that is practised in groups of one. But it is not easy for spirituality to flourish when you are on your own. It can help to pray with other people, whether the prayers are formal, extempore or silent. A group in prayer creates an atmosphere, which encourages each member to pray. Being with others aids worship too. As other people come into the presence of God you are drawn along with them. Learning about the faith with others provides stimulation and encouragement. The larger entity creates a context in which the individual can encounter God. Take away that context, and it becomes harder to develop your spirituality... while there is certainly a place for personal prayer and study, there is little future for solo-spirituality done purely on your own...[3]

But isn't prayer supposed to be private?

Some would like us to believe that Jesus taught 'solo-spirituality' as the only legitimate expression of prayer, and they reject the idea of public prayer gatherings or a call to collective fasting. Certainly the Sermon on the Mount was a clear slap in the face for the blow-your-own-trumpet religious contortions employed by the Pharisees. And the Pharisees were big on outward show. They dressed to make a religious fashion statement, adorning themselves with tephillin (small leather boxes containing portions of Scripture) and tassels – the four tassels from the prayer

---

[3] Michael Moynagh, *Changing World, Changing Church* (London: Monarch, 2001)

shawl. The message was screamingly obvious: 'Hello every-one, look at me, listen to me, I pray, I give...'

We do know that there was a small area in the Temple – hidden away – called the Chamber of the Silent. It was there so that the embarrassed poor could go for help without the identity of the helper ever being revealed. But the problem was not with the public *context* of the Pharisees' prayer and fasting – rather it was the smug, self-preening *attitude* with which they entered the public arena that provoked Jesus to open fire.

If public spirituality is forbidden, then Jesus broke his own guidelines with a ministry of the miraculous that was so blatantly in the public arena; and the early church, in their corporate gatherings, misunderstood him too. What Jesus is talking about in the Great Sermon is the pride that strikes when the public is about – the obsession with being noticed.

My good friend Gerard Kelly sums up this peacock-preening piety incisively

Some pray like a BMW,
7 coats of shine and shimmer masking the hardness of steel
With an anti-emotion warranty to guard against the least
    sign of trust.
Some pray like a Porsche.
0 to Victory in 6.7 seconds
Banking on the promises of pray as you earn prosperity.
Jesus recommended praying in the garage, with the door
    shut,
Engine and radio off,
Praying when no-one is looking, forgetting the traffic of the
    day, meeting God in the quiet lay-by far from the pray
    and display.[4]

---

[4] Gerard Kelly, *The Games People Pray*

Naturally supernatural

One of the best ways to develop a corporate atmosphere
of prayer together without falling into the trap of pride-
ful piety is to develop a natural feel to our praying.
Prayer that is conversational, simple, that does not
invoke a drum roll – or roll of the eyes – that says, 'Oh,
gosh, we're *really* godly, aren't we?', is the prayer that
pleases God and keeps us away from deadly Pharisaism.
We should be able to walk down the street together and
ease into a conversation with God in a way that doesn't
suggest that we've either lost our sanity or obtained a
PhD in religiosity.

Develop a culture of gratitude in your church and
your friendships – and not just for food. And on the subject of 'saying grace', avoid the subtle trap of being
religiously non-religious! I know people who have
rejected the practice of giving thanks before eating
together because it can descend into a hurried mantra
that actually is irritating. The food gets cold and the
wooden prayer is just a monotonous litany that contains
a momentary nodding awareness that there are millions
who won't eat today. But those who react against this, in
their insistence that religious rituals can lose any sense of
reality and heart, now religiously *don't* say grace, and get
rather appalled at anyone who does. 'Say grace? Are you
serious?' A new religious habit has been formed around
what we *don't* do.

Give yourselves to *seasons* of special prayer in your
church. Right now in Timberline Church, Colorado,
where I hold a teaching post, we are holding a forty day
period of prayer for the 'prodigals' – those who once
were living as believers but who are no longer walking
with Christ. Find a prayer partner; or get into a prayer
triplet. Friends of mine have formed a prayer triplet that

meets weekly on the South Downs of England to pray for West Sussex. Rain, shine, or icy snow, they are up on those draughty hills faithfully every week. They conclude their evening of prayer by heading down to a local pub in the village to enjoy a couple of beers. When I visited the pub, the landlord had no idea that I knew them or that I was a Christian. Pulling me a pint, he nodded over at the group in the corner. 'See those blokes over there, mate? They're Christians, you know...' I braced myself for the expected oh-what-a-bunch-of-drips-and-they're-hypocrites-too speech. It never came. His face a broad smile, the landlord continued. 'Every Monday night, whatever the weather, they go up on the hills to pray for Chichester. Marvellous, isn't it? The whole village knows who they are. It's great!' I spent a few happy evenings by the log fire in that pub participating in chats that the whole bar was a part of – conversations that included God, the gospel, the church – without awkwardness or embarrassment.

The awesome power of agreement

Dallas Willard points out that the church is a community with *request* at its heart; we are people who have been appointed by God to petition him together. Through Christ we have been granted the privilege and confidence to be a requesting people.

When we learn to agree together, we bring the filter of community to our requests; we can check and confront each other, and prevent the meandering up selfish back roads that can happen when the request is known only inside one head. In agreement, we can encourage one another in persistence and tenacity, spurring each other on to continue in the place of request. And we can bear one another's burdens in the place of agreed request, encouraging each other relationally even as we do battle spiritually.

Agreement together can bring the generations together across the church too. So often we can be tempted to hive off to our generational stylistic preferences – we gather around our stated worship and music expression, rather than the centrality that we are one in Christ. In a way, we are setting ourselves up for the calamities that visit any church that is consumer driven.

Change your church

Perhaps you are frustrated right now, a little angry even, because you know that the church of which you are a part does not have natural, heartfelt praying as part of its culture. Avoid the temptation to start talking and thinking about *them*. I notice that when our church does something right, we use the word *we* or *us*, happy to align ourselves to the outfit when it's doing well. And when weakness is diagnosed, we like to step out of it for a moment, preferring to refer to the group as *they* or *them*, distancing ourselves from the church's weaknesses and shortfalls. But the church, in both its strengths and weaknesses, is us. Like it or not, we are contributors individually to what it has become collectively. The *they* people usually become self-righteous scourges of the church, self-appointed pains in everyone's necks – don't do it!

Own responsibility, and seek to bring prayer into your relationships. Some will roll their eyes and think that you are being pretentious – don't feel the need to defend it, or give them a lecture on their own gross carnality! Little by little, the practice of celebration, gratitude and request can be introduced into the little cultures that all of us create – and the church is changed as a result.

4

Believe that you're not welcomed by God

'Our *Father...*'

> *'If you want to judge how well a person understands Christianity, find out how much they make of the thought of being God's child, and having God as their Father. If this is not the thought that prompts and controls their worship and prayers and their whole outlook on life, it means that they do not understand Christianity very well...'*
>
> Jim Packer

My dog thinks that I'm the antichrist. His name is Arnie (named after Arnold Schwartzenegger; it seemed like a good idea at the time). He has a chocolate box face that melts most hearts, the straggly, floppy ears gifted to all Cavalier King Charles spaniels, and he views me with the affection that one might feel for a serial killer. So why this sniff of disdain, this haughty silent rejection treatment that cats are expert at but dogs emulate quite well? After all, I've taken him for at least ten walks in the last five years (don't alert the RSPCA – we lash him to a treadmill every morning. *Not really*). And I am occasionally the one who opens the huge sack of beef scented rabbit droppings that constitutes his food supply. Still he hates me.

I thought about taking him to a dog psychiatrist, but I can't figure out how that works. What do you say to a dog with possible psychological problems? 'So, tell me, how long have you been feeling like a dog?' Anyway, I've managed to work out why I am so low in Arnie's pecking – or barking – order, without the assistance of a canine clinician. It's all about *negative expectation*. He has instinctively established that a telling off is inevitable when I'm around. I'm always the one who tells him to get down when he jumps up at the legs of our guests when they come into our home. It seems to me that one should be able to visit friends without having a furry black nose snuffling all over you. So I tell him off. He obediently desists, and then settles himself down on the feet of the now-seated guest, as if to say 'I don't know you at all, but I really like you. But as for *him*...' If dogs could spit, mine would.

And so, whenever I call his name, he gets up and walks woodenly to his basket. It doesn't matter if I make demented grandpa cooing noises, click my fingers in welcome, purse my lips in a friendly whistle, or even sit there gently toying with a five-pound slab of steak. Arnie hears my voice, and has convinced himself that the sound of it is an overture for a telling off. Off he goes, my warmest offer of fuss and affection rejected again.

Forgive the parabolic illustration from the friendship (or lack of same) betwixt my dog and I, but I want to use it to provide a backdrop for our look at a few more myths about prayer. The issue, once again, is that of negative expectation. Some of us don't even bother to try to spend time with God, because we're convinced that the possibility that he might say something to us probably means that we're going to get a good telling off.

Surely the One who is ablaze in awesome holiness couldn't say anything other than 'could do better?' Prayer inevitably becomes a chore, because it is viewed as a frosty chat with a snooty headmaster who is bound to mark our test papers by scrawling a huge 'F' all over our lives.

There are plenty of people who think that God is a never-pleased taskmaster. It's reported that John Cleese recently confessed that he'd love to be a Christian, but he couldn't pass the exam. But this is the gospel reversed. Yes, God can be hugely demanding. But he is also the One who, while pointing out the weaknesses of, say, the seven churches in the book of Revelation, was also able to commend them with a hearty 'well done!' Some of them had worked hard, pursued truth, and stayed faithful in suffering. And the risen Jesus congratulated them for it.

If we're ever going to get deeper into prayer, we must first realise that an encounter with God does not necessarily mean that it's another bad news, 'get in your basket' type of meeting. Can we believe for the possibility of heaven's congratulation and affection, the promise of the One who calls himself Love? We are welcomed people. This answers the great inquiry of lonely humanity.

Do you love me?

That is the nagging question that gnaws away inside each and every one of us. This prevailing question mark is what fuels much or even most of the activity that we call life. The question waits quietly in the wings, prompting a persistent, aching longing. Are we loved?

The joint, as Fats Waller would have said, was jumping... and during the last set, the saxophone player took off on a terrific solo. He was a kid from some insane place like Jersey City or Syracuse. But somewhere along the line he had discovered he could say it with a saxophone. He stood there, wide-legged, humping the air, filling his narrow chest, shivering in the rags of his twenty odd years, and screaming through the horn, 'Do you love me?' 'Do you love me?' 'Do you love me?' And again, 'Do you love me?' 'Do you love me?' 'Do you love me?' The same phrase unbearably endlessly and variously repeated with all the force the kid had... the question was terrible and real. The boy was blowing with his lungs and guts out of his own short past; and somewhere in the past in gutters and gang fights... in the acrid room, behind marijuana or the needles, under the smell in the precinct basement, he had received a blow from which he would never recover, and this no one wanted to believe. Do you love me? Do you love me? Do you love me? The men on the stand stayed with him cool and at a little distance, adding and questioning... But each man knew that the boy was blowing for everyone of them...[1]

There is a sure answer to the agonising query, and it is a definite yes. But how can we humans, stumbling and fumbling around in the dark as we are, know that love? We may hear that there is a God whose name and primary identity is love, but where are the tokens and expressions of his love to be found? We can catch a whisper of romance from creation. Extravagant sunsets seem to carry the signature of a loving artist who nightly signs off the day with the flourish of a fluorescent pen. Towering mountains point towards more than cold

---

[1] James Baldwin adapted from Donald W. McCullough, *The Trivialization of God: The Dangerous Illusion of a Manageable Deity* (NavPress, 1995)

design, and boom the deep bass resonance of solid, dependable love. The fingerprint of the Lover is clearly stamped across everything that he has made. And yet we all sometimes wonder: is all of this just wishful thinking? We need a clearer message, a more certain herald of love. Thankfully, God has *demonstrated* his love in the giving of his Son, and *described* that love in the Scriptures. And he has planned that his church be a *working model* of lives lived in tune with the symphony of that love.

In the inspiration of his word, God apparently likes to use superlatives, to write his love notes in language that is arresting. He employs them repeatedly throughout the New Testament to let us know just how valuable we are to him. There we are lovingly told that we belong to a royal priesthood, and that we're the honoured citizens of a new, holy nation. We are a people who belong to God, his prized, delightful possessions. We are uniquely God's workmanship (the word comes from the Greek *piome* – poetry). Why the shower of superlatives? Certainly the Lord is not in the habit of throwing cheesy platitudes about like a heavenly greeting card writer, in a sad attempt to cheer us up for a second or two; he really is in the serious business of letting us know that we're priceless. God is not into mere precious moments and superfluous, superficial backslapping. We are greatly loved.

But we find it difficult to believe that all this wonderful news – good news indeed – is actually true of *us*. We are prepared to nod in mental assent to the idea that God generically loves his church; and we concede that there are other, far more Christian people than us out there that really are the apple of Jesus' eye. But not us. No, we who are treated to a relatively uninterrupted view of the mucky dungeons of our inner lives can never feel that our cold cells could echo with the footstep of the Great

Lover coming to *us*. Mother Teresa maybe. And all those ancient devotional types who dressed in hair shirts, drew blood with pious whipping, and refused to wash because of the pleasure that is water cleansing the skin – yes, those serious, and sometimes barking mad people of yesteryear – they were keen enough to merit love. And maybe old Mrs Smith with the planet eclipsing hat who wears her fingers to the bone knitting psychedelic tea cosies for distant sweating missionaries – yes, she must be loved, what with all that knit-one-purl-one-knit-one-purl-one for Jesus down through the years. And that slightly odd chap who *always* raises his hands during the worship – and the notices too, he's *really* keen. But me? Not likely.

I have experimented with this theory of mass self-rejection that is hip amongst evangelical Christians. March into a large meeting, take upon yourself a glazed eyed prophet-at-large look, and announce in thunderous tones that God has hereby spoken with you in the prophetic Robin Reliant on the way to the service, and that he has revealed unto yourself the *specific identity* (*first and last names, and also the colour of their front doors*) of some parishioners present who have been guilty of GREAT NAUGHTINESS – shout loud enough – and watch everyone duck. When it's time to call up volunteers for the death row of public judgment, most of us live with a lingering suspicion that *our* name is the very next one to be called. Christians line up with the downcast recognition that they are surely to trudge the Green Mile of shame.

Try the same procedure in reverse. Soften your voice, allow a warm glaze to come over your eyes, and announce that, verily, the old Reliant did reverberate with the booming voice of the Almighty, who was muchly in the business of letting you know the identities of some

people present who God hereby says are *wonderful, fantas-
tic, faithful glorious lovely disciples of his*. Check out the
audience. None of them are ducking, fearful; no whitened
knuckles grip the pews now. No, everyone is peering
around the place trying to figure out whom on earth these
divine bouquets are being delivered to. And most people
think that the flowers can't possibly be for them. How can
he really love me?

A friend who is going through a turbulent time
emailed me just this morning. With permission, I share
her painful dilemma

> Have you ever wondered if you were really saved? The
> thought occurred to me in the middle of last Sunday serv-
> ice. I cannot believe for myself that God really loves me as I
> am. I can believe it for others but I can't seem to grasp this
> ever important teaching. So the thought was if you can't
> believe the whole thing how can you only believe part of it
> and still be okay? And do you think God is punishing me
> for these thoughts? Just look at me. My marriage is hanging
> by a thread, what kind of mother would have a screaming
> child and what kind of pastor's wife would end up doing
> time in a mental ward? Is this redeemable? And do we
> really have to do Christmas this year?

A missionary – and missionaries are obviously known
for their high levels of commitment to and sacrifices for
Jesus – wrote of her lingering feeling that the God who
loves the world might stop short of liking her

> Our inability to develop a truly God-shaped set of expecta-
> tions easily could leave us wandering out the forty years
> or so of our adult lives in our own self-made desert
> wilderness. In my case, the greatest consequence of long-
> term, misplaced expectations has been their deadening

effect on spiritual vitality. I questioned God, myself, my circumstances... God must not love me the way He loves others, I thought. I must be on Jesus' blacklist. I guess I'm just one of those Christians that God can't use...[2]

All of this obviously has devastating effects on our ability to pray. Why would we even bother to try to draw near to the One who we are sure will reject us? Some of us don't pray because we don't feel welcome, and we couldn't be more wrong. When Jesus taught his disciples to say 'Our Father', he was not just laying out a protocol for entry into the divine presence, or an opportunity for us to let God know who he is. 'Our Father' lets *US* know who God is. And Jesus' teaching on this was not without cost, as radical as it is. The pagans used to address God as Father, but Jews were not in that general habit, mainly because the Fatherhood of God is not a central theme in Old Testament biblical theology. And so Jewish prayers would focus on the multiple titles of sovereignty, and the Lordship, glory and grace of God; it must have seemed somewhat outrageous to hear Jesus and his disciples talking about God as Father. But he insists that we know that we are welcome. For some, this seems just too good to be true.

Good good news

Most of us have been taught a philosophy of suspicion: 'if the deal looks too good to be true, then it probably *isn't* true' ... 'There's no such thing as a free lunch'... 'Everyone has to pay their own way', and even the oft-quoted but utterly unbiblical 'God helps those who help themselves.'

---

[2] Carol Kent, *Secret Longings of the Heart* (NavPress, 1990)

As children, those of us who were blessed enough to be raised in a positive, safe environment are most likely to be at ease with the idea of grace and receiving gifts. I know that my children never protested when they were given a chocolate bar, never exhibited any concern that perhaps they might be unworthy of the gift, and were not in the habit of asking me if I had made the mortgage payment that month, therefore confirming that I could afford to give them the aforementioned confectionery. As children, their hearts were uncluttered with all inhibitions about receiving, and without a further word the chocolate disappeared down their throats at the speed of light.

But the dawning of adulthood and so-called 'maturity' can bring with it the death of our ability to receive easily. Our coming of age can signal the end of many great attributes of childhood, such as innocence, hope, play, adventure, and imagination; our sense of ease when we are the recipients of gifts can shrivel as the years pile up too. Try giving a gift to some people when (a) it's not Christmas or their birthday – and therefore it is not anticipated or expected and (b) when they have no opportunity to give you something back – therefore the generosity cannot be reciprocated. You may find yourself observing a major crisis. 'You shouldn't have. I don't know what to say. I didn't get you anything. I feel so embarrassed…'

There have been millions of Christians who have operated their whole lives in this sense of embarrassed crisis when it comes to the freely given grace of God, so they stay out in the cold; shivering strangers to the wild welcome party that the Father throws for us all, if we will only come inside.

The early church fathers could hardly believe this concept of fatherhood; it seemed like too good a deal to be true.

They added a tentative preface to the Lord's Prayer, a hesitant peek around the corner to see if it was okay to run into the arms of God. 'Grant that we may dare to call on Thee as Father' was their nervous prayer. It was as if they were saying, 'Can we really do this?'

They were wrong in their hesitancy, but perhaps entirely right in the addition, sensing as they did the hesitation that flutters in most human hearts when God invites us to call him Father. But the alphabet of Christianity starts with F for Father – not failure. Many Christians today – leaders included – wrestle with the stunning notion that heaven's courts might roll out a red carpet of welcome for us. No wonder prayer is not frequently associated with laughter – or joy of any kind. And when that is our lot, we will be more at home with tears of remorse than laughter or fun.

McDonalds intercession: instant agony

I was standing in a minister's office, ready to go into a meeting where I would preach. Everyone looked bright, happy, positive – until someone suggested that we should pray for the service in general and me in particular. What happened in the next three seconds would have provided a wealth of material for a psychological study of evangelical spirituality. In an instant, everyone around me burst into tears (there were no actual tears, just the sound of much wailing and crying) as each person came mournfully into the presence of a God who they assumed must surely be irritated with them. There is of course a time to cry, but this fast-food style of intercessory wailing freaked me out. And as soon as the prayer bit finished, everyone stopped sobbing, brightened up and began an immediate discussion about the

football results. If my children burst into crocodile tears
every time they saw me, I'd be very worried. Perhaps
insecure shepherds pass on their own toxic insecurities
to their flocks?

I occasionally visit church buildings where there are
'altar benches' or 'mourners benches' placed at the front
of the building, purpose-made furniture for penitents,
with boxes of Kleenex thoughtfully provided. I'll concede again that there is certainly a time to weep as well
as laugh, and that some who come forward for prayer
are distressed because they're walking through valley
times of serious difficulty or grief, and therefore the tis-
sues are a thoughtful addition. But I am nervous of the
implication that to come into the presence of God means
that tears are the likely result; unless, of course, we are
rediscovering a sense of awe. Now that would be welcome, tears and all.

Missing it: the Father for my perfect future

Some of us live under the deception that *one day* we will
be welcome in the presence of God – when we're less sinful, more mature, more accomplished in service. Our
welcome is in the future, but the present is blighted with
a sense of banishment. It is obvious, yet needs to be said:
if we are waiting to be whole before we venture into
friendship with the healer, we will never pray, barred
from the courts of God by yet another pervasive myth.

There is a mad irony in the idea that we have to come
to God strong and whole, and therefore back off from
him because we're not; he is the physician offering a
clinic for the sick. In his teaching on prayer, Jesus made
an opportunity to seek forgiveness a central and pivotal
part of the prayer act, encouraging us to ask that our

debts might be forgiven – but more on that later. The irony is further compounded by the fact that the more enthusiastic believers are the ones who feel their sinfulness most keenly (their desire to please God is heightened, and their conscience with it), and in their zealous shame they run from the God who gathers the Mephibosheths, those who are invited to the party despite being acutely conscious of their emotional and spiritual disabilities.

Missing it: the Father for my past

Then there's the subtle deception that somehow God has loved me in the past alone – that his love rose like a huge wave when Jesus went to the cross to die for my sins, and that there love was poured out and, in a sense, was spent. This locks God's love up in history and turns it into a noble fossil, an emotional antique. Calvary was indeed the crowning work of grace, but it was not a one hour fleeting wonder, a brief flush of romance. God didn't just love us in terms of an action of the past, *he is and remains* love in his very nature and make-up, right this very second. That means that everything he thinks and feels and does is entirely consistent with his primary DNA, which is love. And that means that there is a heart at the core of the universe that beats quickly about you, now. One writer puts it well, and not merely sentimentally:

'If God had a refrigerator, your picture would be on it. If God had a wallet, your photo would be in it.'[3]

---

[3] Mark Stibbe, *From Orphans to Heirs* (Oxford: Bible Reading Fellowship, 1999)

That is true of the God of today – and of the you that you are today as well. The huge torrent of love that God felt towards you, even at the precise moment of Jesus' death – (he knew of you back there, before you were born), is the massive love he feels and has towards you this very second, even as your eyes scan the typeface of these words.

Soren Kierkegaard prays thus

You have loved us first, O God, alas! We speak of it in terms of history as if you loved us first but a single time, rather than without ceasing. You have loved us first many times and everyday and our whole life through. When we wake up in the morning and turn our soul toward you – you are there first – you have loved us first; if I rise at dawn and at the same second turn my soul toward you in prayer, you are there ahead of me, you have loved me first. When I withdraw from the distractions of the day and turn my soul toward you, you are there first and thus forever. And we speak ungratefully as if you have loved us first only once.[4]

Claiming it: Grace for now

Grace cannot be measured, metered or contained any more than we can cup the universe in our hands. It is scandalous, abounding, explosive – and, in a sense, dangerous; in that we can misuse it. Perhaps it takes a forgiven slave-owner like Newton to be allowed to use the word 'amazing'.

Consider the mad mathematics of grace...

---

[4] Richard J. Foster and James Bryan Smith, *Devotional Classics* (San Francisco: Harper San Francisco, 1993), p107

People are prepared for everything except for the fact that beyond the darkness of their blindness there is a great light. They are prepared to go on breaking their backs plowing the same old field until the cows come home without seeing, until they stub their toes on it, that there is treasure buried in that field rich enough to buy Texas. They are prepared for a God who strikes hard bargains but not for a God who gives as much for an hour's work as for a day's. They are prepared for a mustard-seed kingdom of God no bigger than the eye of a newt but not for the great banyan it becomes with birds in its branches singing Mozart. They are prepared for the potluck supper at First Presbyterian but not for the marriage supper of the lamb...[5]

Grace announces the verdict of God that seems like insanity to our cool, but fundamentally flawed logic. Godfrey Birtil, a gifted worship leader, heard me coin the phrase 'outrageous grace' in a teaching session. He went off and wrote a song by the same name, and has been in deep trouble ever since, the recipient of frosty letters and acerbic post-meeting 'I just want to say this in love, brother' comments from people who are offended at the word 'outrageous' being used in connection with the grace of God. I have encouraged him to stand firm. 'Grace', as Philip Yancey says, 'is the message that the world is waiting for. When it comes, the world will be silent before it.'

Karl Barth, the world famous theologian, arrived at the University of Chicago to deliver some lectures, and was asked by the press what was most profound truth

---

[5] Frederick Buechner, *Telling the Truth* (San Francisco: Harper & Row, 1997), p70, quoted in Philip Yancey, *What's So Amazing About Grace?* (Michigan: Zondervan, 1997), p62

he had learned in all his years of study. Barth thought for a moment, and then responded: 'The deepest and most profound truth that I have ever discovered is this: Jesus loves me, this I know, for the Bible tells me so...'

But like the Prodigal, wrestling in the hug of his father and still desperate to deliver his 'I'm not worthy to be called your son, make me like one of your hired servants' speech, we resist the idea of outrageous grace poured out on *us*. We are the descendants of super-wrestler Jacob, whose prayer was 'I will not let you go until you bless me.'[6] But our wrestling turns his prayer around on its head. 'I will not let you bless me, let me go...'

God: not our *natural* father, but adoptive by choice

Mark Stibbe, himself an orphan whose life was wonderfully transformed by an adopting family, has written a warm and beautiful book about the biblical truth of adoption.[7] He claims that the struggles of the Reformation wonderfully recovered the great truth of justification by faith, but that this is basically the language of the courtroom. So God is portrayed as judge; a judge appeased. A crime – the sins of humanity – is paid for in full by the shed blood of Christ – but God remains the judge nonetheless. But there is a further lost treasure in the New Testament that leads us, as Stibbe says, 'from the language of the courtroom to the language of the family room.' This 'ultimate blessing of the Gospel', (Jim Packer's description) is the truth that

---

[6]	Genesis 32:26

[7]	Mark Stibbe, *From Orphans to Heirs*

we, who are in Christ, have been formally adopted into the family of God. God has only got one *natural* Son – his name is Jesus, and he is and has always been the Son. But now our 'big brother' Jesus has laid down his life for us, opening the way for smeared, sinful us also to find a way into the Father's house, not as cringing servants, but as sons and daughters. Stibbe makes a very moving and powerful point when he reminds us that children who are adopted often go through a very precise choice and selection process: they are received into a family because they were specifically chosen to be so selected. The good Fatherhood of God, the sufferings of his Son and the message of his grace and adopting love must be at the heart of our churches if we are to live with a sense that we are welcomed into his presence – and so can draw near to God's throne with confidence.[8] Stibbe also says that a worship song written some years ago by Ishmael was part of the trigger process that brought him into a new found sense of God's wonderful adopting love

> Father God I wonder
> How I managed to exist
> Without the knowledge of your parenthood
> And your loving care
> Now I am your son
> I am adopted in your family
> And I can never be alone
> Cos Father God you're there beside me
>
> I will sing your praises... for ever more.
>   Ishmael[9]

---

[8] Hebrews 10:22
[9] ThankYou Music

Fatherhood and the prayer experience

Fatherhood is not optional in relationship to our spirituality; Jesus insists in his teaching that we use the
language of family when we come to God in prayer.
When we approach God, he will not let us be content
with addressing him as Lord, King, Sovereign, Creator –
or even simply as God. He is, of course, all of the above,
and yet insists on being *more* to us than all of these. To
come to him as merely God or Lord is to enter into dialogue with him on the basis of his *power* and the extent of
his reign – but makes no reference to his *relationship* to us
and ours to him. But every single time we use the word
'Father' we celebrate and remind ourselves that we are
his, and he ours: every prayer becomes another family
reunion. And the insistence that we call him Father takes
us beyond the God-as-my-vending-machine mechanics
that can characterise some praying, and draws us once
again, not just to the Potentate of Potentates, (though that
he surely is) but to a warm bosom of love. He simply will
not let us shout our prayers from a distance. Every time
we utter his name, we remember that we are home, and
that we are his children.

Once our family relationship has been established, our
calling him 'Father' also reminds us that we come to One
who is able to change things – he has the power; that he
offers us insight from his vantage point – he has the wisdom. As children we are freely invited to bring our requests
without hesitation. Again, this flies in the face of our
human experience, where we might have been scolded by
our human parents because of our incessant begging for yet
another chocolate bar or another unneeded toy. And yet we
serve a God whose only complaints in this respect seem to
be about our *not* asking, or when our asking has an obses-
sive selfishness at its heart.

> When you ask, you do not receive, because you ask with wrong motives, that you may spend what you get on your pleasures...[10]

The invitation and command to come to him as Father establishes a protocol of communication – neither the distant, formal speechmaking that one might use when addressing a King, nor the matey chumminess that one might use with a friend in the pub. Our privilege is to know intimacy without flippancy.

Greater expectations

The more time I spend around Christians – and indeed as I delve into the mysterious inner space of my own heart – the more I conclude that most of us have fairly low expectations of what it means to be in friendship with God. We are like the returning Prodigal, who could only hope for a menial job and a square meal from his father's hand. 'Make me one of your hired men'[11] was his practised liturgy. And, come to think of it, his logic was reasonable. Hadn't he effectively treated his father as dead when he demanded his inheritance – even though his dad was still alive and well? And hadn't he then turned around and blown the whole lot on a wretched lifestyle that he knew would have broken his father's heart? Based on the human calculations that we are all surrounded by, logic said that a servant's job would be the very *most* that he could anticipate; indeed, he could well be sent packing with an empty stomach and a parental flea in his ear.

---

[10] James 4:3
[11] Luke 15:19

But our small thinking about him does not box in God. He has been assaulted and caricatured by our small doctrines, and the result is a perception of a pernickety, mealy-mouthed God who is more like an obsessive-compulsive chartered accountant (apologies to members of that fine profession!) than a wildly generous dad. God has been disguised, his beauty masked. Perhaps that is why Dietrich Bonhoeffer said that the church's main task is to 'wash the face of Jesus', to remove the religious grime with which he has been smeared – most often by the church – over the years. The real shining face of Jesus will be, to many, irresistible – if they could only get a glimpse of it. With some startling words and some overstatement, one writer says

The Messiah whom Jesus' contemporaries expected – and likewise any and all of the messiahs the world has looked to ever since… are like nothing so much as the religious version of 'Santa Claus is coming to town'. The words of that dreadful Christmas song sum up perfectly the only kind of messianic behaviour the human race, in its self-destructive folly, is prepared to accept: 'He's making a list, he's checking it twice, he going to find out who's naughty or nice' – and so on into the dark night of all the tests this naughty world can ever pass.

… Jesus… is not, thank God, Santa Claus. He will come to the world's sins with no list to check, no tests to grade, no debts to collect, no scores to settle. He will wipe away the handwriting that was against us and nail it to his cross (Col. 2:14) He will save, not some minuscule coterie of good little boys and girls with religious money in their piggy banks, but all the stone broke, deadbeat, over extended children of the world whom he, as the son of man – the Holy Child of God, the Ultimate Big kid, if you please – will set free in the liberation of his death... he tacks a 'Gone Fishing' sign over the sweatshop of religion, and for all the debts of all sinners who ever lived, he provided the exact change for free. How nice it would be if the church could only remember to keep itself in on the joke...[12]

The Fatherhood of God – it's the basis for our confidence in prayer, and it's the celebration message the world is quite literally dying to hear. I like Capon's analogy of the 'joke'. How wonderful it will be when more of those, deeply saddened and depressed by Satan's morose trinkets, hear the infectious sound of our salvation laughter.

12 Robert Farrer Capon, *The Parables of Grace* (Grand Rapids, Wm. B. Eerdmans, 1988)

5

Believe that God is a long way off

'Who is in the heavens...'

*'Everything is enwrapped in love, and is part of a world
produced, not by mechanical necessity, but by a
passionate desire.'*
                                              – Julian of Norwich

Jesus teaches us to pray to our Father who is in heaven
– or so most translators would have it. But what does
that mean? Is God up there, aeons away – and we
stranded down here? Is prayer a *very* long distance
phone call?

From a distance

Bette Midler and Cliff Richard have both produced
what is *musically* one of my favourite songs: *From a
Distance*. I often find myself humming the lilting
melody, much to the consternation of my family who
are more than convinced that God has called me to sing
as much as he has called me to be a male model; in other
words, not at all.

But I've come to the conclusion that, singable though the song is, it actually reflects a very subtle heresy that has caused the church and the world all kinds of untold grief: that 'God is watching us – *from a distance.*' The idea is prevalent. God is the 'old man is the sky', or 'the man upstairs.' Wherever he is, the notion goes, he isn't here. Even if we're willing to concede that he may well have been here in the past – in creation and incarnation; and if we go so far as nodding to the idea that he might well just stop by in the future – in his second coming – we can still conclude, totally wrongly, that in the meantime he has effectively checked out. There are devastating results from that kind of 'God out there' thinking. Firstly, wicked human behaviour runs riot: after all, there is no power, no moral guardian in close proximity, is there? God is, at best, consigned to the realm of the hereafter, managing the business of heaven, and that will take care of itself – post death. Surely, the average Briton asserts, if there is a God, then any kind of judgment after death will be little more than a raised eyebrow and then a free pass to heaven will be handed over; it'll all be all right on the night – or the day – of judgment. But in life today, he's not to be considered or reckoned with now, because, on a planet wide basis, the Sheriff's out of town. Party on, cowboys…

But the 'from a distance' approach to God's proximity affects our praying too. The idea that God is 'our Father in heaven' can suggest that he is located somewhere out in the wild blue yonder, perhaps slightly to the left of a distant solar system. Prayer thus becomes an exhausting attempt to fire missiles into the dark, to throw snowballs at the moon. At best, we will feel like those scientists who constantly beam radio signals into deep space in the hope of a response from some passing extra terrestrials some day – hardly a recipe for a warm relationship.

Worse, it deteriorates into an emotionally sapping experience if every time we come to worship and prayer, we are quite literally reaching for the stars.

> Some think that God is a Wizard of Oz-type being sitting in a location very remote from us. The universe is then presented to us chiefly as a vast empty space with a humanoid God and a few angels rattling around in it... of such a 'god' we can only say good riddance. It seems that when many people pray they do have such an image of God in their minds. They therefore find praying psychologically impossible or extremely difficult. No wonder.[1]

Hell's marketing campaign

There is dark design behind a marketing campaign designed to discredit God. Satan has consistently committed himself to the work of slandering God; the strategy goes back to Eden, when the question fashioned to undermine God's character was hissed: 'Has God really said?[2]

The slander includes pumping out the message that God is absent; and indeed the campaign has worked well, in introducing the ultimate barrier to keep a Holy God distanced from his beloved created humanity – sin. *Sin* was and is the wall of estrangement, (the 'dividing wall of hostility') which Christ came to demolish[3], not just to alter our ultimate destination, but to reconnect us with our God *now*. Sin serves Satan well; hell wants us to believe, if we will believe at all, in a God fractured from his creation,

---

[1] Dallas Willard, *The Divine Conspiracy* (London: HarperCollins, 1998)
[2] Genesis 3:1
[3] Ephesians 2:14

a departed God. The madness of temptation comes to us, not only to smear us with shame and defeat, but also to corral us away from God and into the despair that comes with that estrangement. In short, it's a very bad deal indeed.

Then there is a second banner message in the wicked campaign to discredit God: that is in the propagation of the idea that he is impotent – or that, if he does have any power at all, he's not inclined to use it nor to lift a divine finger to help *us*. That's why we sometimes feel such a sense of surprise when prayer is actually answered. And, like Old Testament Israel, we are quick to forget his acts of deliverance and kindness. Indeed, we tend to forget what we should remember and remember what we should forget. God is thus portrayed as distant and disinterested. Couple this campaign with the general idea that God is geographically distant, and the result? We, humanity, feel lost in space. Permit me to quote Willard again

> The damage done to our practical faith in Christ and in his government at hand by confusing heaven with a place in distant or outer space or even beyond space is incalculable. Of course God is there too. But instead of heaven and God always being present with us, as Jesus shows them to be, we invariably take them to be located far away, and most likely, at a much later time – not here and not now. And should we then be surprised to feel ourselves alone?[4]

Grieving for God

When my dad died – he became a Christian in his last few years of life – I learned a very simple lesson about the nature and reason for the grief that I felt.

---

[4] Dallas Willard, *The Divine Conspiracy*

The hollowness and overwhelming sense of loss that I experienced was not provoked by the idea of death itself – because I knew that, in Christ, he was now alive. The problem was that he was now *alive elsewhere, departed.* When Christians lose loved ones they are often unhelpfully told by Christians friends that they should not be sad or grieving, because this person is with Jesus now – and that was precisely my problem. He *was* and *is* with Jesus and therefore somewhere else – and that meant that he was and is not with me. Permit me to say that there are times when I want my dad back here, now, with me, drinking a cup of tea from his favourite mug, and waxing eloquent as he did on everything that moved. Grief says: come back. I don't want you to be somewhere else in the universe, even if it is paradise there. No wonder the spiritualists pack in the crowd, offering as they do a bridge from here to there, a link to the other side – even if God clearly warns us[5] not to set foot on that weak, dangerous and deceptive bridge.

Indeed my dad is elsewhere. But I think that we can limit God to being in that area of the heavens too, and thus we experience a similar grief for God, believing him to be exclusively in that elsewhere domain. Thus we believe that God is alive, to be sure, and even active in some remote, distanced way – but not alive here now, with me.

The disciples began to taste that grief with the growing knowledge that Jesus was going away – but he immediately encouraged them with the news that an-other comforter, the Holy Spirit, was coming.[6] They would never be abandoned or forsaken, never again be alone[7] in the universe. He is here.

---

[5] Leviticus 19:31

[6] John 14:16

[7] Matthew 28:20

Compounding the problem: Come, Holy Spirit

This idea of the absent God can be fuelled by a misunderstanding of the charismatic practice of asking the Holy Spirit to come, particularly in a renewal service context. Personally, I have no problem with praying such a prayer, but we must clearly understand that we are not asking God to be where he was previously not, and therefore to come down. To do so would imply that we need another Day of Pentecost every time we come together. Surely, when we ask the Holy Spirit to come, we are asking him to *manifest himself*, to *make his presence felt*. He acts and works generally where he is welcomed, and in praying for his coming we are rolling out the red carpet for him, and inviting his activity among us. But we are not asking God to fill a vacant space that was hitherto empty. Such an idea leaves us to walk out of those meetings to a returned state of felt emptiness and abandonment, and it obviously overstates the value of those gatherings. God becomes a localised deity who lives in the church car park: and that he is certainly not.

The reality: God, everywhere, all powerful – and here

So what does Jesus mean when he teaches us to pray 'Our Father – in heaven'? In his gospel, Matthew uses the term 'Father in heaven' twenty times. One commentator suggests that our problem – the suggestion of a God who lives above – has been created by a poor translation of the word heaven, which he insists should be the plural *heavens*. Suddenly, everything changes. Far from suggesting the Father is distant, Jesus teaches precisely the opposite. The 'first' heaven, biblically, is the atmosphere or air that immediately surrounds your body. Jesus is teaching us here that God the Father is in all and is all in all; right near us, and right out there both. He is introducing us to the infinite, omnipresent Father who is so very, very close, and in whom we 'live and move and have our being.'[8]

Matthew is also giving us wide-screen vision of the Lord, banishing our dwarfed godlets with the revelation that we have a Father whose authority and presence stretches across the heavens and the earth. And this truth is far more than abstract theology, but reaches down into our Monday morning praying. It means that we have authority to participate in the unfolding drama of history-making, as we partner with God through our praying.

Love does make the world go round

God is near. That affects our understanding of the world around us. We have evolved an idea that there are 'laws' of nature – which seem to imply that there is a cold-hearted mechanic, or nerdy scientist at the heart of the universe. Nature becomes not an ongoing act of creation and sustenance, but a machine of necessity. James Bryan Smith writes of his discovery that there is a passionate artist at the centre of it all – not that he was but is no longer interested, but that he is actively splashing his paint and moulding his clay all over the place.

> G.K. Chesterton changed the way I look at the world around me. He pointed out that nature is not a system of necessity. Yes, the sun will probably come up tomorrow, but it need not. Perhaps each day God says to the sun, 'Arise!

---

[8] Acts 17:28

Go forth!' Yes, grass is typically green, but it need not be. God could make it purple if he wished. There are no 'laws' of nature. Frogs jump and birds fly and water runs down hill not because of laws but because, writes Chesterton, God wishes them to do so...[9]

Divine graffiti

It's been said that most of what God does, he does behind our backs. We all like to give the impression that we know what God is doing; most of the time, we haven't got a clue. Once in a while, we catch a hint of his work, shout loudly our brilliant discovery, and probably dash off another book about it. God is near, but he doesn't always consult. In other words, he is at work in a billion ways this very second that we cannot even fathom. It is a grave mistake, for example, to see mission as something that starts in the initiative and heart of the church – that leads us to exhausting, sweaty effort. Rather, our task is to connect with that which God is already doing in *his* mission, the *missio dei* – mission of God. And sometimes God's fingerprints are to be found in the most unusual places. One writer sums it up so wonderfully: 'God is constantly at play across the earth.'

He is very much here, and not only when he is acknowledged or noticed. That helps me to understand why a piece of gloriously inventive music may be written by someone who doesn't know God; I can admire the masterful use of colour and shade on canvas, the work of an artist whose heart is in the far country, and yet who has been kissed, though he doesn't know it, by the touch of the

[9] James Bryan Smith, *A Little Handbook of God's Love* (London: Hodder & Stoughton, 2000), p15

Creator. Shall I ascribe the source of their creativity to
Satan? I will not, because we are living in a God-bathed
world. I caught a glimpse of his inspiration when I
watched the film *The Truman Show*. Jim Carrey – Truman –
bumps into the edge of his artificial world. He didn't know
it, but he had spent his whole life in a reality that was false,
because it was a huge television studio. Like *The Matrix*,
Truman discovers that there is a bigger reality beyond the
artificial confines of the studio. Will he walk through the
door to the real life – or will he listen to the dark voice that
taunts him: 'There's nothing more out there, Truman'? Will
he continue to play the myth-game? The whole world
cheers as Truman walks through the door into true life.
Was God listed on the movie credits? On the contrary. But
I reckon that he was making his presence felt in the craft-
ing of that film; the invisible director and scriptwriter,
prophetically prompting the questions of life through art,
scribbling his signature in unexpected places.

God – very much here, and our provider

The immediacy of God also says something to us
about our approach to the provision of our daily
needs. Jesus paints a portrait of a close-up God who is
actively involved in every detail of life on the planet.
He is revealed as the One who knows us intimately;
knowing what we need before we even ask him.[10] The
fact that God not only can be known, but that *he knows
us* is foundational to biblical revelation. To each of the
seven churches of Revelation, walking as they did
through a dark season of pressure, with the clouds of
persecution gathering on the near horizon, Jesus says

---

[10] Matthew 6:8

'I know.'[11] We are therefore not designated as impersonal digits or numbers in a database, lost in the crowd, but each of us stands as known by God. Again, his knowledge of us and his closeness to us leads us to expect and anticipate his hand at work in daily provision for our lives.

> Therefore I tell you, do not worry about your life, what you will eat or drink; or about your body, what you will wear. Is not life more important than food, and the body more important than clothes? Look at the birds of the air; they do not sow or reap or store away in barns, and yet your heavenly Father feeds them. Are you not much more valuable than they? Who of you by worrying can add a single hour to his life? And why do you worry about clothes? See how the lilies of the field grow. They do not labour or spin. Yet I tell you that not even Solomon in all his splendour was dressed like one of these. If that is how God clothes the grass of the field, which is here today and tomorrow is thrown into the fire, will he not much more clothe you, O you of little faith? So do not worry, saying, 'What shall we eat?' or 'What shall we drink?' or 'What shall we wear?' For the pagans run after all these things, and your heavenly Father knows that you need them. But seek first his kingdom and his righteousness, and all these things will be given to you as well. Therefore do not worry about tomorrow, for tomorrow will worry about itself. Each day has enough trouble of its own.[12]

Concluding: the God who dwells with us

As we draw this discussion on the close-up God to an end, we must remember that the very foundation of the

---

[11] Revelation 2:2,9,13,19 and 3:1,8,15
[12] Matthew 6:25-34

Christian faith is an invitation to live in, abide in, and rest in the here and now presence of God. Without him we really can do nothing[13] – and his closeness and dynamic activism in our lives is the only way that we can experience real transformation. We may tinker and mess around with the external behaviour and bits of our lives, but only he can get inside us, and work a work of true change. He is at our side. C.S. Lewis reminds us that, fundamentally, we are but 'tin soldiers'

> Our faith is not a matter of our hearing what Christ said long ago and trying to carry it out. The real Son of God is at your side. He is beginning to turn you into the same kind of thing as himself. He is beginning, so to speak, to 'inject' his kind of life and thought, his Zoe [life], into you; beginning to turn the tin soldier into a live man. The part of you that does not like it is the part that is still tin.

God is not the One who is watching us from a distance, scarcely hearing or understanding our shouts and sobs. On the contrary, you, right where you are, right now, are hemmed in and surrounded by your loving heavenly Father. And so Saint Patrick prayed

> Christ to protect me today
> against poison, against burning
> against drowning, against wounding
> So that there may come abundance of reward.
> Christ with me, Christ before me,
> Christ in me, Christ beneath me, Christ above me,
> Christ on my right, Christ on my left
> Christ where I lie, Christ where I sit, Christ where I arise,

---

[13] John 15:5

Christ in the heart of every man who thinks of me,
Christ in the mouth of every man who speaks of me
Christ in every eye that sees me,
Christ in every ear that hears me.[14]

Breastplate Prayer of St Patrick

---

[14] The works of St Patrick from *Ancient Christian Writers: The Words of the Fathers in Translation*, translated and annotated by L. Bieher (New York: Newman, 1953), p71

6

Believe that prayer is just about you

'Hallowed is your name...
Your kingdom come, your will be done, on earth,
as it is in heaven...'

*'We have de-clawed the Lion of Judah and made him a
house cat for a pale priest.'*
— *Dorothy L. Sayers*

Beware low flying cornflakes...

I am sad to confess that Kay has banned me from watching certain Christian television programmes. It would be churlish to mention which, but this viewing prohibition has been so ordered because she is weary of the sight of breakfast cereal dripping down the front of the television set. Why is it that some of my hottest moments of boiling rage centre around these anonymous programmes? Yes, I'm irritated by the occasionally facile, 'Jesus wants me for a Barbie doll' philosophy that seems inherent in this stuff, and I feel pastorally aggrieved (what a high sounding description for my anger!) when I hear preachers take a slick approach to suffering and hand out slogans rather than Scripture. But I think that my frustration is mainly provoked by the message that seems to be pumped out with cereal-wasting regularity: that the Gospel is all about *me* getting *my* dreams fulfilled, and using Jesus for that purpose.

Jesus becomes Santa with a cross. The idea that I might be called to lose my life[1], of signing up to make his kingdom my first priority, seems lost. This kind of approach to Christianity, with its easy formulas and slogans, trivialises the sublime, and reduces the Lord into a cosmic vending machine, urgently plied with intercessory tokens when you spot that new car you'd like. Worst still is the notion that if you're not rich, or grinningly healthy, then somehow you're spiritually blighted – another slap in the face for the vast majority of the world who won't eat today. Now, not only are their stomachs empty, but their hearts are second-rate too, cursed as they are with a poverty of faith – or so the absurd notion goes. Vomit-inducing stuff.

Pray: not a mechanistic formula for *me*

I admit to being nervous of the 'Seven laws for blessing in your life' approach, simply because it is so impersonal, and I don't believe any relationship – including one with God – can be reduced to laws and abstract principles. There is no real intimacy, no foundation of love and laughter; just a process towards a result, a means to an end. It centres on the gift rather than the Giver, and treats God like a heavenly supermarket check-out operator.

But as we hear Jesus begin to talk about God's Name being hallowed, and his kingdom and his will breaking

---

[1] Matthew 10:39

out in the earth, we discover that, when it comes to requests, we do find ourselves second in line.

No neutral spirituality

We are scarcely a sentence into the model prayer of Jesus, and we immediately bump into the rule, reign and authority of God. We have barely tiptoed into his presence, and suddenly we have to acknowledge the reality of a moral and spiritual power that is beyond ourselves. There is a popular spirituality that is available today – perhaps it's always been available – that comforts us, helps us to realise our dreams or to discover our cosmic significance, but that makes absolutely no demands upon us. It only brings solace; no sacrifice is involved. It involves us finding the 'god' of our choosing, one that we ultimately can make in our own image. This god is superficially lovely rather than intrinsically loving, in that it will never challenge our selfishness, hedonism or greed. But Jesus refuses to allow us to make him into our good luck charm, a divine rabbit's foot or any other kind of talisman.

If we will come to him, we will come as those willing to see his rule and order as the very first priority in our lives. But let's remember, if that sounds a little too harsh and austere, as if there is a cold control freak at the heart of the universe, that God brings order *because* he loves. What kind of loving father would sit silently in the face of hellish chaos breaking out in the lives of his children, without wanting to restore the order and peace that his rule can bring? We quickly collide with the truth of his kingdom reign, yet not the rod of iron gripped in the fist of a dictator, but the storm-calming rule of peace ushered in by the greatest Father there has ever been.

God's kingdom rule is good – the best. To live under it is liberation and joy – if that is not the case, then how can we really pray sincerely that others will come under it? What prisoner would hope that others would get to experience the damp, near-starvation of the cell, and torture at the hands of his guards? He would be mad so to pray! No, the good rule of the Good God is breathtakingly wonderful. As we taste that, we can hope and pray that others will find it too.

The priority of his Name: let it be hallowed

Talk of names being 'hallowed' is foreign to our ears; indeed, our most likely familiarity with something being hallowed is probably *Hallowe'en*, the eve of All Saints' day of old. God's Name *is* holy, and won't become more holy because of our prayers. Rather, in asking that God's Name should be *hallowed*, we are asking that his Name might be seen as worthy of respect and honour – a lofty prayer indeed in a culture that has demoted the Name of Jesus Christ to the level of the swearword. In ancient times much importance was invested into a name – indeed the Name of God was so revered that we really don't know how to pronounce *Yahweh* properly today. A person's name was synonymous with their reputation and character: to defame someone's name was serious indeed.

It goes without saying – yet we must own the tragedy of it – that God's Name has been consistently misrepresented, maligned and smeared – and, though it gives me no pleasure to confess it, this smearing has often been because of our foolishness. As a result of our poor advocacy, he has been found guilty without a trial. He has been dismissed as irrelevant because we, the church who

profess his Name, have so often disguised him as tedious
– mainly because we have been so unappealing. This
was no small feat for us and our churchly ancestors –
taking the most brilliant, luminous personality in the
history of the universe, dulling and dumbing him down.
But, alas, we have done it, and done it all too effectively.

Dorothy L. Sayers laments the damage done to the
Name and the Person of Christ

> The people who crucified Jesus did not do so because he
> was a bore; quite the contrary. He was too dynamic to be
> safe. It has been left for later generations to muffle up that
> shattering personality, and surround him with an atmos-
> phere of tedium. We have de-clawed the Lion of Judah and
> made him a house cat for a pale priest.

But all is not lost: we are those who are also privileged to
say, 'Your Name be hallowed.' Perhaps this is the prayer
of *alarm* that a child might feel if someone suggested that
their parents were dishonourable. We pray all of this
prayer as children to *Abba* Father, not just the introduc-
tion to the prayer.

When I was in secondary school, there was a particularly
noxious chap who used to be acid-tongued with his insults
and derision. In any war of words, his favourite tactical
insult was 'Your mother is a prostitute'. He used the insult
so frequently that one might conclude that half the school
was the offspring of ladies of the night. As we might expect,
that particular sneering accusation always signalled a black
eye for him; he could say whatever he liked – but tarnish the
honour of our mothers? Break out the bandages. You would
have thought that he would have learned. He spent most of
his schooldays looking like a badger.

I'm not too sure about those folks who go around
tersely correcting everyone who blasphemes or misuses

the Name of Jesus. It seems to me that the end result
of the rebuke might not necessarily lead to any positive
fruit – but I entirely acknowledge that there are times
(perhaps), when we have earned the right and it might
well be appropriate to protest when the Name of the One
that we love is maligned and misused. But surely our
prayer that the Name of God should be honoured goes
deeper than concern about swearing. We are praying
that the lost will discover the life that is only available 'in
the Name'. When God's Name is defiled, the signpost
that can lead the wandering home is defaced and van-
dalised.

This Name is the source of salvation, and we pray that
the real truth will come out about it and the One who
owns it. Notice that our prayer is immediately focused
outward, towards a dark world. Why? Because God
weeps for the emptiness of the wandering and longs that
the signpost of his Name might be cleaned up. In a post-
modern age of pluralism and relativism, we must hold
on to the biblical insistence that life is only available in
one Name. By it alone can those stranded in sin's bliz-
zard come in from the cold.

Andrei Bitov is a Russian writer who describes the
day he found that warm welcome

In my twenty seventh year, while riding the Metro in
Leningrad, I was overcome with a despair so great that life
seemed to stop at once, pre-empting the future entirely, let
alone any meaning. Suddenly, all by itself, a phrase
appeared: without God life makes no sense. Repeating it in
astonishment, I rode the phrase up like a moving staircase,
got out of the Metro and walked into God's light.[2]

---

[2] David Friend, ed., *The Meaning of Life* (Boston: Little,
Brown, 1991), p194

A brief excursion into a question?

Praying that is closeted away from the pressing needs of
the world isn't worth a lot; mission is quickly at the heart
of the praying that God smiles upon. Before we have
said anything else much, we have been invited to look
outward to a world that defames the Great Name. We
have looked upward, to 'Our Father in the heavens' and
then immediately we look outward at the lost world that
is so loved of the Father.

Forgive the question but... whatever happened to
evangelism? Yes, I know that over a million in the UK
have been through Alpha, an unthinkable idea twenty
years ago; but as I travel throughout Britain, I don't
often hear Christians talking about great opportunities
that they have had to share Jesus with someone. Have
we lost the ability to reach out? Have we devolved the
responsibility that we have for sharing about and
introducing people to the Jesus who has so changed
our lives to Alpha (which is undeniably a wonderful
gift from God to our nation at this time)? We learn here
that our church gatherings should be totally linked
into the pulse of what is happening beyond her clois-
tered walls. Church was never designed to be an
escape act, a trip to a spiritual Disneyland that enables
us to forget the hurting, wounding world in which we
all live.

Lynn Green painfully shared recently about a charismatic meeting that he attended just a few miles from
Bethlehem, while the infamous siege raged on, in which
a number of lives were lost. Palestinians – including a
number of Christians – were being shelled by Israeli
tanks. Just a few thousand yards away, Christians got
together for another Holy Spirit top-up without any reference to the blood and tears that were being shed so

close to where they met. Spirituality that turns its back on the world isn't worth any time or effort.

The priority of his kingdom and his will: let it come

We are blessed with the authority to say, 'Your kingdom come, your will be done', which are words often misunderstood to refer exclusively to the second coming of Christ, and our future in the eternal kingdom of God – the proverbial pie-in-the-sky-when-you-die thinking – though why anyone would equate the hereafter with a pastry crust is quite beyond me. The confusion is compounded further by Matthew's use of the term, 'kingdom of heaven' – which again causes us hastily to conclude that he is talking about something that will be totally *later*. In reality, Matthew's use of 'kingdom of heaven' is simply because he was writing to Jews and using the common Jewish terminology of the day. The other Gospels avoid this term because it would have been meaningless to the ears of Gentiles.

In short, I want us to see that *praying that the kingdom come* is about what's going on today and on Monday morning – *and* it's also about the ultimate future. One day the fullness, consummation and totality of God's kingdom reign will be found in the return of Christ, but, in the meantime, we are able to call for the kingdom of God to break out today through a thousand different apertures. A smile in the office, a moment of kindness at the school gate, a comment that brings light into darkness in the college corridor, the calling for a zebra crossing in that accident black spot – in these moments, as we call for righteousness – the right order of God – to prevail, so the kingdom relentlessly ripples outward...

Let's take a moment to explore the kingdom a little more – it's a neglected theme, but it's so core to our praying – and our understanding of where we fit in God's purposes.

Recovering the kingdom...

The 'kingdom' was the main teaching theme of the ministry of Jesus. The heartbeat of the Sermon on the Mount is found in the command that we 'Seek first the kingdom of God.'[3] Jesus' travelling preaching and teaching ministry had the kingdom as its core theme – he went about 'preaching the good news of the kingdom.'[4] Michael Green remarks 'the kingdom was Jesus' prime concern.' Matthew uses the term thirty-two times. So how come we haven't heard more about the kingdom from our pulpits? Dr I. Howard Marshall echoes this concern about kingdom silence when he points out that in the past sixteen years, he has only heard two sermons specifically devoted to the theme of the kingdom of God... despite the fact that New Testament scholars all agree the kingdom of God was the central theme of Jesus' teaching. It is a tragedy that we have subdued the kingdom shout of Jesus – and have subdued it to the faintest whisper.

The kingdom: the arena of his reign and rule

The biblical words for kingdom are *malkuth* (Hebrew) and *basileia* (Greek). The meaning carried by these words is primarily that of 'rule' or 'reign' rather than

---

[3] Matthew 6:33
[4] Matthew 4:23

'realm'. In other words, when we speak of God's kingdom, we are thinking about the arena of his rule and command, rather than any kind of located geography. Perhaps that's why our minds struggle; we are familiar with the idea of a king or queen reigning over an area of land – their geographical *kingdom* – rather than thinking of a kingdom in terms of the area of their rule and influence.

The term 'kingdom of God' does not appear in the Old Testament directly, but the long-awaited kingship of God was the hope and theme song of the prophets. God was seen as king over Israel and also over the whole earth – but the Old Testament also speaks of a day when he shall *become* king.[5] That's a helpful illustration of the 'it's here, but there's more' truth of the kingdom. God is already king, but he will yet be king in greater fullness – in the fullness of time!

And then… the odd bloke in the wilderness shows up

John the Baptist, alarmingly noticeable with his odd fashion choices and his worrying habit of snacking on grasshoppers, suddenly came on the scene and lobbed a verbal wake-up call at his listeners. 'Repent, for the kingdom of heaven is at hand.'[6] He came in the line of the Old Testament prophets, standing on tiptoe, proclaiming that the kingdom was about to come among them – and so a radical response of repentance was required from those who listened to this oddest of preachers. John conducted much of his ministry in the desert, traditionally the place of restoration for Israel. The message was bubbling –

---

[5] Isaiah 24:23; 52:7; Zephaniah 3:15; Zechariah 14:9ff
[6] Matthew 3:2

something or somebody very, very big was about to step onto the stage of human history. And then he came.

Jesus and the kingdom

Jesus arrived preaching the same message as cousin John, but with the added phrase, a stick of dynamite for John's wake-up call: 'the time is fulfilled.'[7] John had spoken at the eleventh hour – but with Jesus, the clock struck midnight! In the synagogue, he says '*Today* this scripture is fulfilled…'[8] Already the messianic banquet had begun. It was a time for feasting not fasting, the bridegroom was here, and the new wine was flowing. The disciples had seen an age that the prophets and kings longed to see.[9] The new age was here![10]

Wherever Jesus went the kingdom broke out, in all of his words and works. Demons were driven out, sure evidence of a clash of invisible kingdoms. The territory of the false king-pretender, Satan, was being pushed back as, like a relentless avalanche, the rule of Christ rolled out with a thunderous roar.

The kingdom – it's all about *you*, Jesus

The kingdom has never been about a distant monarch or impersonal rules and regulations – as we saw in the last chapter. Rather, the kingdom of God was present for

---

[7] Mark 1:15
[8] Luke 4:21
[9] Luke 10:23,24
[10] Matthew 11:2-6; Luke 7:18-23

people whenever Jesus was present. As he walked and worked, the kingdom came.[11] The religious leaders of the day made the same mistake that we are tempted to walk into; they were looking for other 'stuff' and signs to announce the kingdom's arrival, but failed to spot the King among them. We can do the same, as we get over-enamoured with the signs of the kingdom; the gifts of the Holy Spirit, healing, deliverance – wonderful and vital though all these are – or when we reduce our Christianity into an impersonal moralism, a Christless Christianity that knows how to be good, but knows little of the touch and whisper of God.[12] There is no kingdom without the king of the kingdom being present through the Spirit of God!

Kingdom RSVP

Unlike the warrior kingdoms of men, where kings' rules are extended through bombs and bullets, the kingdom of God comes as it is received. It is at hand – it is within the grasp of all who hear the proclamation, and there are many who today are 'not far from the kingdom.'[13] As we respond willingly to the invitation, we are invited to step into the banquet life now.

Nothing is more important than our response to the kingdom rule of God. It should be our first priority of business in life, item number one on every agenda.[14] As we humble ourselves, we become part of it.[15]

---

[11] Luke 11:20
[12] Luke 17:20
[13] Mark 12:34
[14] Matthew 6:33
[15] Matthew 18:1-4

But what about the church?

The church is *not* the kingdom of God. This is not just a theological detail, but a vital fact – when we confuse the church with the kingdom we get the idea that God only works in the realm of the church, like a localised deity who lives on the church car park, to use an illustration I used earlier. Thus he is cut off from the real world, and only acts in the cloisters of the church – a tragic misunderstanding!

As we've seen, the kingdom of God is the sphere of the dynamic rule and reign of God. But the church is the *primary agent* of the kingdom. God extends his kingdom in all kinds of ways; he will, at times, directly inter-vene in people's lives; he whispers and shouts through creation, but the main method that he has chosen to extend the kingdom is through a visible, working model of kingdom life: his church.

Sometimes the model works well – and sometimes it's a hideously damaged array of grinding, clashing cogs and wheels that is the worst possible advertisement for the Good King. So, as we live and announce that there is a new rule to live under, that we are now subjects of another Master, so we have the ability to draw others to kneel at the throne of love – or perhaps to run from it, if our demonstration is bad. In this way, the church holds the keys of the kingdom[16] and carries the awesome responsibility of opening and shutting the kingdom to others. The breathtaking truth is that as you and I go about life, we are carriers of the kingdom – and represent it either well or badly. When the disciples travelled from town to town, those who encountered them came 'near to the kingdom of God.'[17] Again, this is more than

---

[16] Matthew 16:19; 18:18
[17] Luke 10:8-12

theological musing. All of us – without exception – carry something called *influence*. The way that we use that in our day-to-day lives will affect the view of others, not only of us, but also of the kingdom that we represent. We can leave impressions that last a long, long time – even eternally, either for good or for evil.

We are not only influencing others in the formations of their opinions about us, which, let's face it, are not that important, but in their opinions about the effectiveness of the Great King. They will judge him as they look at us. Just as Israel was called to be a 'light to the nations', so the church is designed to be the visible expression of what it means to live under a new rule – the reign and authority of God. When we become part of the kingdom, we discover a new community of fellow subjects; and so entrance into the kingdom means participation in the church.

That will be costly, because we, the church, are on the journey but we painfully know the truth that we have not arrived yet. We should therefore never be surprised at the imperfection of the church – just as we have not yet breasted the tape, neither has she. Just as the kingdom is both 'now' and 'not yet', so is the church. She belongs to two ages. She lives in the current age of sin and destruction, but she also belongs to the age to come – of better things ahead, so she is called to model this truth through humility, mercy and forgiveness.[18] It is the duty of the church to display a shop-window of the future; in an evil age of self-seeking, pride and animosity, she lives out the life and fellowship of the kingdom of God and the Age to Come. So 'kingdom living' is an essential part of the witness of the church – she is not just a *proclaiming* community, but in her lifestyle is a *demonstrating* community.

---

[18] Matthew 7:1–5

Let your kingdom come: How will our prayers be answered?

As we draw this brief look at the kingdom to a close, we must ask this question. As we pray, 'Let your kingdom come' – how will that happen?

The kingdom breaks out as the message of the gospel is clearly announced. The gospel of the kingdom – the wonderful news that through the death and resurrection of Jesus, the power of the enemy has been broken, and that we can experience freedom as we receive the message – this is the message of the church. We call people to come in repentance – the number one requirement for entering the kingdom – to the king himself, whose rule is open to anyone who lays down their rebellion. We call people, not just to a sinner's prayer, but to the handing over – the loss – of their whole lives in order to place those lives under new lordship.[19]

And then we are called to demonstrate the power of the kingdom. Jesus operated through both proclamation – announcing the good news – and demonstration – healing the sick and casting out demons. The disciples carried out the same dual role of healing and deliverance; they too cast out demons and healed the sick.[20] Their power was delegated, yet they operated in the very same power that had worked through Jesus. So the conflict between the 'gates of hell' and the kingdom of God will continue through the ministry of the church in the same way as it was in the life of Jesus.

This demonstration will not only be in the supernatural: as we echo God's heart for social justice, we begin to express the values of the kingdom, as the poor,

---

[19] Mark 8:35
[20] Matthew 10:8; Luke 10:17

the oppressed and the downtrodden suddenly find themselves blessed in Jesus' new order of things.

We must hold unswervingly to this kingdom message. As it is preached and modelled across the earth, 'then the end shall come.'[21]

And all this means... what?

As we pray, 'Your kingdom come', we immediately bump into a few important realities. First, we realise what the church is actually for: contrary to our consumerist ideas, the church is not here for me at all – it is here for the release of the kingdom. Our obsessions about whether we like the music/the colour they painted the church's kitchen/the preaching style/the type of tea bags we use fade into irrelevance. The church is not here to serve us or particularly please us. It is here to serve the king and his purposes. And then – our church programme and structure is not of the highest importance. The issue really is: what programme or structure will serve the purposes of the kingdom? We pray for a kingdom mentality towards change in the church.

Understanding the gospel of the kingdom will prevent us from being tempted simply to lock people up in church activity; we will want to release them to be part of those who fulfil their call to seek first the kingdom of God, in whatever sphere they find themselves. More about this in the next chapter.

The truth of the kingdom helps us avoid parochial praying for our church. Indeed, our primary prayer is not for the blessing of one or indeed all of the churches in the area, but rather that the *kingdom might come*.

---

[21] Matthew 24:14

And understanding something of the clashes between the kingdoms of light and darkness gives us a focus for spiritual warfare.

The kingdom teaches us to be patient in prayer – and fellowship! We are already aware that we live with a tension of the already but not yet, and so we live knowing that the actual is not the ideal. We work with the actual but do not let go of the ideal: we are neither pessimists nor unrealists!

We do not look for the restructuring of society along a 'biblical model' as have some, because our kingdom is not of this world; but we do look to be 'salt and light' within society, so transforming our environment as the goodness of God's kingdom touches lives.[22]

The kingdom becomes our priority. Let it come.

The church gets into trouble whenever it thinks it is in the church business rather than the kingdom business. In the church business people are concerned with church activities, religious behaviour and spiritual things. In the kingdom business, people are concerned with kingdom activities, all human behaviour and everything which God has made, visible and invisible. Church people think how to get people into the church, kingdom people think about how to get the church into the world. Church people worry that the world might change the church, kingdom people work to see the church change the world![23]

---

[22] Some of this material is adapted from Martin Scott's *'The Kingdom'* – *Equipped to Lead*

[23] Howard Snyder, *Liberating the Church* (Wipf & Stock, 1996)

7

Believe that prayer can never be about you

'Give us today our daily bread'

'When Parliament is in session, no man's property or reputation are safe.'

Okay, we've established that the ever-tempting spirit of selfishness shouldn't hijack our prayers. The problem is, stop reading this book now and you'll be cowering away from the possibility that you could pray about your own life and all the stuff that makes it your life. And you'd be wrong. Jesus, having given us the priority of the kingdom, invites us to share our daily needs, worries and indeed all of the scattered paraphernalia that makes up our today – with the God who has decided to be interested.

God is interested

The thought hit me like a truck: why on earth does God seem to view prayer – us talking with him – as so very important? What's the big significance about us having what often seems like a one-way conversation? Is God lonely and in need of company? Perhaps our hurried answer to that question would be *no*. We rush to consider the God who is without need, who is surrounded by the glories of angelic courts and who lives, as one writer puts it, 'a very interesting life' in his interaction with creation. I do believe, however, that as the core fabric of who God is, is love, then there *is* a sense in which he longs for us and for our friendship. I hesitate with this; some preachers have portrayed the Jesus who stands at the door and knocks as some kind of poor chap out in the cold who is desperate to be let in – a picture I reject as a distortion of the biblical portrait of Christ at the door. And yet to love is deliberately to make yourself vulnerable and in need of the one that you love. A friend of mine shared how he had gone through an extended time of spiritual barrenness when he had found little time for prayer. His testimony was that when he returned to God, the Lord whispered, 'I missed you.'

God is interested in us and in all our stuff. It's important to remind ourselves of this, lest we begin to see prayer as a spiritual activity that needs to be done, well, simply because it needs to be done, a bit like the spiritual equivalent of brushing our teeth twice daily. When we treat prayer like this, it becomes a task without purpose, except that we feel that we have 'done the Christian thing' by engaging in it. The beautiful news is that, in a world where we can feel lost in the crowd, a mere digit in the great, overflowing database called Earth, there is One who wants to listen to us with genuinely avid interest. We've all known the disappointment of sharing something sensitive and deep with another, only to watch their eyes glaze over as their available quota of interest in us has apparently run out. Yet we, without pompous self-absorption, all want to be known and heard. There is something wonderful about the ability within a vintage friendship to take the lid off the confused inner space inside of our heads and peer inside, hand-in-hand with that friend. God is interested; there will never be a yawn in heaven when you pray; the Amen to conclude the chat will always come from you. And his interest is not to be reduced to a forensic, information-gathering kind of interest. Rather, he desires to entwine himself into the woof and weave of our daily lives.

Request and conversation

Allow me gently to look at an area that gives me some concern – the idea that prayer is designed to be a two-way conversation, a dialogue with God. I worry lest we end up disappointed that we don't have this dynamic interactive encounter going every day – and that we assume that everybody else does and that therefore we should. Let me say immediately that I know that God wants to speak to us; that as we read Scripture and meditate upon it, as we walk the dog, work at the office, listen to the prophets, hear the preacher, the voice of God is there to be discerned and heard. And of course, the whisper of God can be found directly in times of prayer. I'm just not convinced that prayer is designed to be some fluid, flowing conversation between us and heaven – and the few that I've known who confess to these constant 'I said and then God said' matey chats as their experience have, quite frankly, worried me; I have even pondered the unthinkable and wondered about the robustness of their mental health. As I look at the Lord's Prayer, it seems to me that it is primarily about what is really a one-way conversation with us coming to God and leaving our worship, our fears, our sins and our requests there with him. What delight comes when we sense his immediate response; and yet we should not feel rejected if we come, we speak and that's it. I've no doubt that we would hear more if we would be still more; and surely there are some understandable and unfathomable reasons for our not being able to discern more of his voice. Yet we can come, pray and know that we are heard, whether or not we feel the psychological comfort of an immediate response.

God bless me

The Prayer of Jabez has been nothing short of a publishing phenomenon. Millions of copies have been shifted and the attractively presented little book by Bruce Wilkinson has spawned a whole family of merchandising spin-offs. So far I haven't seen *Jabez* boxer shorts, but, in marketing terms, there's still time.

The concept is simple – an encouragement to ask God to bless *me*. And what's so very wrong with that idea? We are quite wrong when we refuse to ask God to do anything for us at all. We touched on this earlier, but let's use it again; perhaps most of us struggle with the idea that God might want to bless *us*. Of course, he wants to heap gifts on dear old Mrs Bloggs who has baked cakes to raise dosh for the missionaries every Friday for the last three hundred years and God *definitely* wants to issue heavenly credits to Mr Whatsisname who, faithfully and without complaint, sweeps up the cigarette ends around the back of the youth hall. We wonder if Mr Whatsisname is really an angel who disguises his wings well beneath a threadbare brown caretaker's coat. But God wanting to bless *me*? With all my mixed up motives and prayers that send me, and probably a few heavenly beings, off to sleep and heartfelt hopes that our minister (he's a 'lovely brother', but his sermons are as inspiring as watching paint dry) might be struck by lightning if he preaches on for another minute…

Bless *my* soul? Surely not. We know the truth about ourselves only too well to believe that we might be candidates for blessing – as if there is such a thing as one who is worthy of any divine favour.

Perhaps we think that asking for blessing is superficial and selfish. Let's face it, any personal request could be rejected as trivial, living as we do in a world of screaming need. It does seem the height of absurdity to ask heaven to take notice of my headache/bank balance/housing preferences when we stagger daily around the abyss of oblivion.

Yet we serve a Father who chooses to be interested in the tiny lives of his children. Our play, our scuffles and our fanciful hopes and dreams apparently fascinate him. At the risk of sounding sentimental, there is a Dad at the centre of the universe.

And so, while any attempt to reduce prayer to a formula is dangerous and the *Jabez* thing could become a superficial mantra, I think that the encouragement to ask for God's smile is basically a good thing. In fact, I'm thinking about writing *The Prayer of Jeffrey*. It, too, is a simple prayer, but is not based on any obscure Old Testament character – just my own daily experience.

The Prayer of Jeffrey starts like this:

'Heeeeeeeeelpppppp!' Supplicants should note that this intercessory scream is most effective when delivered at a decibel level similar to a passing jumbo jet. The more frantic, the better.

Part two goes like this:

'Heeeeeeeeeellllllllllllllllllllppppppppppppp!' Note the longer, more fervent and indeed desperate sentiment expressed in the prayer. Users of *The Prayer of Jeffrey* may alter this according to (a) personal need (b) mood swing and (c) housing arrangements. Those already blessed with detached accommodation may feel led to yell a little louder than those in semi-detached accommodation. Flat and apartment dwellers might want to skip Part two altogether.

Part three is formed in the manner of a question:

'Is anyone up there?' I include this sentence, as this thought tends to surface most times when I pray. Prayer, for me, often gives birth to a sense of absurdity. The ridiculousness of an earnest, one-way conversation snaps at my heels like a tenacious puppy dog; never really hurting me, it's more a distraction than a menace.

Part four is the gripping conclusion:

'Amen'.

Okay, I admit it, *my* prayer is not going to sell any books, be sellotaped onto anyone's fridge, or indeed produce any hot merchandise but the sentiment is the same as *Jabez*. I need God. Desperately. Urgently. I want to know his smile, sense his hand and hear his voice. So, without apology, I say...

God bless me. And you.

Praying for bread, daily

Most of us are privileged to live in a world of over-stacked supermarket shelves and so the idea of requesting bread to get us through the day is somewhat lost on us. While we should remember that we are in the minority in today's economically unbalanced world and that for many the prayer for some bread daily would be entirely the right request, we can still include ourselves in this prayer. Bread is a symbol for the basic necessities of life. Martin Luther said that 'daily bread' was a symbol for everything necessary for the preservation of this life; as he said, daily bread represented

> food, a healthy body, good weather, house, home, wife, children, good government and peace.

It's rather odd (and telling) that, in compiling his list, Luther put wife and children after good weather...

But for most of us, no angelic delivery service or Elijah and the ravens-type miracle is required in order that our basic needs are met. Why pray for daily bread?

God our security

When we pray about our everyday lives, we are acknowledging that, although we work in order to see needs met, ultimately our confidence and sense of security is not placed in us and our ability to make ends meet, but in God. Internet stock crashes, pension crises and seismic waves in the financial sectors spawned by accounting scandals all point us back to one core source: ultimately God alone can be trusted as provider. That's not to suggest that our labour is not part of the essential provision process; or indeed that saving and being financially prudent about the future are not entirely appropriate. It is just that we see that God is our acknowledged source, over and above all of our best efforts.

This is a healthy prayer, whatever the season of life that we are walking in. When Kay and I returned to the UK having lived in the USA for five years, we faced an uncertain financial future. Having lived comfortably in the USA, we were returning to a promised annual help of just £3,000 (this in 1990) and with no guarantee of anything else. I can remember the feeling of helplessness that overwhelmed me as we took off on the plane bound for England. What would become of us? We had no house of our own, having sold our home in the USA (with a very small profit, not really enough for a down payment on a house in the UK). Interest rates then were at a hideous level of just over 16 per cent and we had rented a flat for an initial period of six months – but then we knew we would have to find somewhere else to live. Property prices were at a booming high.

We *were* able to trust God in that decision and he did take care of us marvellously. But I notice that every now and again I need to look at the balances of our bank accounts just a little too often, somewhat obsessively, to assure and reassure myself that there is enough. When it comes to what we worship, money alone is the one candidate singled out as the main competition with God.[1] Perhaps it's more of a challenge to ask for bread daily in times of plenty than in times of need; but our praying this puts God right at the heart of life: money determines so much about the way that we function.

Nothing mundane in God's eyes

Some early commentators on the Lord's Prayer just couldn't bring themselves to believe that Jesus would 'sink' to discussing something as ordinary and mundane as food. Surely, they reasoned, Jesus was speaking about something deeper, something more 'spiritual' than bread for each day? Early church fathers like Tertullian, Cyprian and Augustine taught that Jesus was referring not to a hearty loaf, but rather 'the invisible bread of the word of God.' Why? Well, surely Jesus is more interested

---

[1]   Matthew 6:24

in Bible reading than toast, or so they reasoned. Jerome thought that 'daily bread' was a reference to the sacrament of Holy Communion. Thankfully, the reformers were more down to earth. Calvin argued that the spiritualising of 'daily bread' was 'exceedingly absurd.'

We too can be guilty of a subtle heresy; that God is only interested in our 'spiritual' lives. Many of us persist in the dualistic idea that Bible reading, prayer and endless hymn singing is watched by God with avid interest, but our reading of a novel, playing a round of golf or anything else 'unchurchy' all register far less on the spiritual Richter scale.

A similar error kicks in when we start talking about 'secular' work, as if those who work 'full time' for the church are doing something *very* useful, but those – face it, most of us – who work in the broader market place are doing something less valuable. The result of this is that we chop our lives up into 'sacred' and 'secular' boxes and feel somewhat schizophrenic as a result. It means that we pray on Sundays for those who teach our children in *Sunday* school, but not for those who teach our children in infant or secondary school five days out of every week. It means that people often demote their work as simply a means to a pay cheque, or an arena for evangelism!

John Stott confronts that kind of thinking

It is very inadequate to see the workplace as having no Christian significance in itself, but only as a well stocked lake to fish in.

The truth is that work, whatever kind of work it is, is part of the creation plan for us – and is not just the result of the fall! We were designed in God's image and so we were designed to be creative and productive as he is.

God works. We are called to do likewise.[2] We work as those who are responsible to God as stewards of his resources.[3] And we are commanded by God both to work and to rest – both are acts of worship.[4]

I have come to the conclusion that the only thing that is secular is sin. Anita Haigh, a friend of mine who did a wonderful job in a very difficult secondary school (and not just because she was a 'good witness!') – calls us away from building those kind of unbiblical boxes

> We must reject views of work which define some roles as more 'spiritual' than others. Biblical characters like Joseph the Egyptian Prime Minister, Daniel the Babylonian statesman, Esther the royal mediator, and Paul the preaching tent maker, had a holistic approach where work and worship flowed together. Some are called to serve in the church, others in finance, education, government, etc. All need respect and support. We are all priests and servants of God together...[5]

Pray about your work, or the need for it if you are unemployed. Make your work a prayer. And stop negating the value of it by rejecting it as less than 'spiritual'.

And praying... daily

I am not in the 'I didn't have my daily quiet time today so God doesn't love me' school. Yet it does seem that the Lord is teaching us that prayer is to be a daily

---

[2] Genesis 1:27
[3] Genesis 2:15
[4] Exodus 20:9
[5] Quoted in 'Novio: Equipped to Lead' teaching session on Christians and the Workplace, by Anita Haigh

commitment, that every new sunrise brings with it a call to bring that twenty-four hour segment of our lives under the loving gaze of the interested God.

My challenge is that I can live on last week's, last month's and sometimes last year's faith. When that malaise creeps into my spiritual walk, gradual erosion takes place in every area of my life. Sin becomes easier to accommodate. Cynicism springs up like a pesky, unwelcome weed. My Christianity becomes more of a moral code or good idea than a love affair. I need Jesus today.

Batteries not included

I was totally exhausted, but had done no real exercise to justify the weariness that was bone deep. Rather, my chronic fatigue was the result of jostling with the crowds of fellow turbo-shoppers who were frantically clearing shelves in the New Year sales. Seduced by the irresistible beckoning of half price stuff, the shops were wall to wall with credit-card-flashing lemmings, desperate to feel the pleasure of purchase now and the pain of payment later. I decided to form an escape committee of one and get out of the madding crowd for just a few minutes. With a sense of relief, I headed into the nearest church – which was also open for business, thankfully, and sat down in the chapel that is reserved for private prayer. The organist was gloriously practising and so I began my reflections with some rather dramatic background music; it was just a little too *Phantom of the Opera*, but certainly gave my praying a hint of drama. The old church smelt reassuringly ancient, the scent of the dust of centuries a welcome change from the clash of warring perfumes in the department store that I'd just escaped.

I scanned the altar, with its beautiful wooden relief: 'Lamb of God, grant us Thy peace'. There were no gold candlesticks; they were locked away, safe from the clutches of any would-be sacred souvenir hunters. The stained glass window above glowed softly with the fading late afternoon light, the old story told in antique Technicolor. Up there, in intricate glass shards, Christ was suspended on the cross, his friends gazing in medieval open-mouthed admiration. He seemed to look down on me, sad-faced, as I clutched my solitary sale triumph; some cut price, bulk purchase dustbin bags.

My eyes wandered to the candle in a wall-mounted votive glass. It flickered bold and strong in the fading half-light, silently driving the darkness back, both in the shadows of the nave and in my own somewhat dingy heart. And then I noticed the mechanical regularity of the flicker and the appalling truth dawned upon me: this was not a real candle, but a neon imitation, a battery-driven fake. No warmth or waxy smoke came from its low wattage neon design, but just a pre-determined glimmer, a rogue light. It seemed so incongruous, as if someone had grabbed a tiny part of a neon hoarding from Piccadilly Circus, shoving it roughly into this ancient place, like a skyscraper in old Rome.

For a moment I was offended for no rational reason. Somehow the electric candle seemed like a cheap trick, an item of ecclesiastical sleight-of-hand. It seemed crass, like a bishop discarding his golden mitre in favour of a kiss-me-quick hat from the seaside. I felt the same emptiness that creeps into my soul when a robotic voice apologises with digital woodenness for yet another late train. Somehow the 'We are so sorry for the inconvenience' speech rings hollow when it comes from a machine with no heart. For reasons that were probably more sentimental than sacramental, the battery-driven candle irritated me.

Then logic arrived and I realised the reason for the hi-tech candle impersonator. I remembered that the days of the sedentary priest were long gone; the amiable round chap with little more to do than prepare a five-minute sermonette was no more. The carefree clerics with bicycle clips of thousands of 'More tea, vicar?' scenes are now an extinct species. In their place are a diminishing army of harassed and hurried priests with a brace of parishes to care for who leap from one morning Communion to another like dog-collared greyhounds... Of course they don't have time to tend the candle, to be popping in every few hours with a genuine wax replacement. The electrical version with a flashing filament is the practical, helpful solution.

And then, having packed my foolish irritation away, I suddenly found myself staring at the pointed finger of personal challenge. Perhaps my entire faith had become like that ever-ready candle; a purposely designed, low maintenance, UPVC Christianity, ruggedly created for my busy, frantic existence where time, or lack of it, prevents me from being able to tend or care for it.

I'm not gifted at tending. My office desk looks like the site of the battle of Armageddon; books and papers are scattered everywhere in the chaos that I try to pretend I like. Our garden, if it were left to my care, would be a useful resource to the Christian church, as a missionary orientation centre for those called to the Amazon. Weeds would flourish in a shocking, choking display; roses would go unpruned and the grass would reach my shoulders. And my car? I couldn't own a convertible; there would so much junk in there that the neighbours would think it was a skip. So many areas of my life suffer from neglect and are terribly unkempt as a result.

I am challenged by the fact that Jesus taught that prayer was a daily exercise; evidence of a desire to live out a friendship with God in twenty-four hour chunks. Living faith, like a living flame, requires nurture, care and attention: too often mine gets overgrown and derelict.

Ironically, neglect is easier if you belong to a lively, energetic church. You can live off the atmosphere of enthusiasm, plug yourself in to the weekly worship drip-feed and remain on cruise control in terms of your own personal spirituality. Add to this an annual trek to a large Christian jamboree, like Spring Harvest (and I totally believe in the value of those events) and you end up with a weekly intravenous experience and an annual event top-up. But hollowness and superficiality lurk within you when Christianity is lived out this way.

A daily note of gratitude to God is evidence of a careful desire to cradle the flame and fuel the fire. Anything truly worthwhile requires energy and effort that will be inconvenient, that will disrupt daily hurry and will cause us to go out of our way to see something really alive develop in our hearts.

Go for authentic, daily faith. Batteries not included.

8

Forget that you're a sinner... and that you're surrounded by the same

'Forgive us... as we forgive'

One of the problems with prayer is that, in a sense, it has become associated with entirely the wrong kinds of people. It is widely believed that prayer is exclusively the habit or hobby of the pious, the saintly, and those worthy of other venerable titles – if indeed such people actually exist outside of the Trinity. Good people, we assume, are the people who pray. This is a dangerous misconception. The Lord's Prayer teaches us that prayer is an activity that is practised only by sinners. Only those who come with a knowledge of their own frailty and incompleteness are welcomed to open their mouths before God. So it is that Jesus has built in an opportunity for us to seek the mercy of God over our sins and our sinfulness when we come close to him. But it seems that, when it comes to the old-fashioned word *sin*, we could lurch to one of two extremes.

The paralysis of cringing penitents

It seems to me that Jesus is not calling us into a navel gazing, obsessively introspective wallowing in our sin;

rather there is a clearly redemptive chord that is heard loud and clear here – the sweet sound of forgiveness. If we come to pray as overwhelmed hopelessly smeared deviants who can only list their catalogue of failures, then we are missing the point. While it *is* useful to be specific about naming and detailing the sins that we are conscious of, we do not do so simply as a litany of despair, heaping up our transgressions and tipping them over our heads like hot coals. Rather, we come in prayer to find the pardon that we so desperately need – and that has been desperately offered. Perhaps it goes without saying – yet we need to be reminded of it – that the provision that God has made for our pardon has been wrought in great bloodshed and tears at the cross. The just pardon that we are granted because of the shed blood of our wonderful big brother, Jesus, has been the most costly purchase and transaction in history! That which has not come cheaply should not be refused or squandered. We can come and tip out the wheelbarrows of our foulest mess-ups, our hopelessly mixed up motives, and break out into the light the most rancid acts of rebellion that have festered in the darkness of secrecy. Dump it all before him, stinking mound that it is.

Failure to understand this will lead us to think that God somehow delights to have us cringe and wince in his presence. One writer, who tragically misunderstood the nature of God, wrote a fearful and yet ridiculous ode to a god who actually doesn't exist, except in the dark caverns of his own fears and prejudices, a god who is a parody of the evil Marquis de Sade

The Marquis de God. Ready to show you how much he cares by punishing you … in a moment of rage, continents convulse with seismic activity. In a fit of moral indignation, he demonstrates the latest craze of viral mutations …

The Marquis de God is simply a god who hates. This is a deity who despises sin and sinners with such passion that he'll murder in order to exterminate them. He forces the noblest creation to dance like a trained poodle on the brink of annihilation. Grace, like a dog biscuit, offered or withdrawn, depending on performance...[1]

The writer is hugely wrong, not least in the very idea of performance-based grace, 'offered or withdrawn like a dog biscuit'. Grace is always on offer, and never on the basis of our performance, but on *his*. Indeed, the performance that we offer, in order to find it, is only in the rebellious act that provoked the need for forgiveness. And so when Jesus calls us to ask for forgiveness, he does so that we might simply recognise our need for help; grace is available – repentance enables us to avail ourselves of it. The call to say 'forgive us', far from being a call to cringe, is in fact an invitation to get up out of our little mud pools and messes and find the exhilarating pardon of God, who is 'My Glorious One, who lifts up my head.'[2]

There is another approach that we can take towards our sin, however. Far from acknowledging and confessing it, we rationalise and excuse it, and rename it as being no sin at all.

Careless fools for sin

In some circles, the very word 'sin' offends, as if it is an antique from the past that has no right to be mentioned

[1] Michael Shevack and Jack Bemporad, *Stupid Ways, Smart Ways, to Think God* (Ligouri, MO: Triumph Books, 1993), pp17ff
[2] Psalm 3:3

in our sophisticated present. We are tempted to rewrite
the moral terms, and change the price tags of the values
of our culture: the lost are not lost, they are 'unchurched'
or more hideously, 'not yet Christians' (a statement
which is stunningly presumptuous about the future
intentions of others).

There is a strong temptation, particularly in our post
September 11th culture, to be nervous of anything that
smacks of absolutes or, worst still, *fundamentalism*. While
I refuse to line up with the word *fundamentalist*, because
it implies an approach to the interpretation of Scripture
that I am unhappy with (and also because most of the
fundamentalists that I've ever met were just that – not
much fun and basically mental…), I am equally worried
about a relentless pursuit of relevance today that causes
us to fudge the issues of what is sinful. I hate legalism
with every fibre of my being – and yet there is a careless
licentiousness that refuses to say that any kind of behaviour is abhorrent to God.

Sin is insanity; to be tempted is to be mugged by a
temporary madness. It is the invitation to sip at a
momentarily pleasant, then devastatingly poisonous
chalice. Temptation brings with it a temporary but overwhelming amnesia; causing us to forget all that we know
that is true; about God, about vows and promises that we
have made to him and others, about earlier trips into
the unsatisfying and shaming trough that is sin, about the
advice given and received at the time from a friend.
The list of the important truths that we blindly forget
could go on. Sin promises liberation, but sets itself to
master us, and carries its own well-worn handcuffs. How
many other people have destroyed their lives, and the
lives of others, as they have been duped by its charms?

To ask for forgiveness is to acknowledge the sinfulness of sin; the spell is broken, the con refused, the

sleeper wakes up. And then, we have to accept God's response...

Letting Jesus wash you

There is a truth that we must grasp if we are to live in peace with a Holy God – without it we might go mad with torment; the agony of the stained living alongside the utterly pure. The truth is that the only ground that we can stand on, if we are to be close to Jesus, is the ground of grace. The pompous, the self-righteous, and those who would blow their own self-assured trumpets must flee as far as possible from him; only those who will sit still and let him wash their grotty, grubby feet are allowed to stay around him.

When Jesus surprised his disciples (grace is always a shock) by washing their feet, Peter represented all of us, and indeed the typical human condition well, by loudly protesting. This was just too good, too kind of Jesus; it was *inappropriate*, or so Peter's mind screamed. But Jesus has always been the utterly inappropriate Saviour, who will always offend the independence of our so-called human dignity with his outrageous grace. To be so treated is nothing short of a scandal, but here's the point: either Peter accepted the wash cloth and the love that it represented, or he would be able to have no part with Jesus whatsoever. When hearing this, Peter, the typical enthusiast, decided that he would have his whole body washed rather than risk breaking friendship with Jesus. As we pray, 'forgive us', we come to One who is armed and ready – with a towel. Receiving the cleansing that we cannot initiate and which we don't deserve is the only basis upon which we can draw close to him. But this is a cleansing that has little to do with merely private piety; it's a grace that we're called to pass around, as we, the forgiven, forgive.

Dallas Willard helpfully points out that we are not just offered grace and mercy by God – but that he offers us *pity* – which, let's face it, offends the very core of our dignity. But this is an important distinction: pity is not just directed at what we do, but is sympathetic to the nature of who we are: at best, sheep. When Jesus prayed for his tormentors from the cross, he sought forgiveness for them on the basis of pity: 'Father, forgive them, *for they don't know what they are doing*.'[3]

> Today, even many Christians read and say, 'Forgive us our trespasses' as 'Give me a break'... this saves the ego and its egotism. 'I am not a sinner, I just need a break.' But no! I need more than a break. I need pity because of who I am. If my pride is untouched when I pray for forgiveness, I have not prayed for forgiveness. I don't even know who I am...[4]

As we forgive... graceless spirituality

It's an uncomfortable thought that has nagged me for years, but it persists: 'Why is it that some folks, who apparently spend lots of time in prayer, are so downright nasty?' I've bumped into Christians who allegedly enjoy a splendid prayer life, but they don't seem remotely to resemble the Jesus with whom they spend so much time. Surely, if their praying were effective as well as lengthy, they would manifest some love, some kindness and grace to others, and even a little humour here and there? Why, if they really do spend so much time in the company of

---

[3] Luke 23:34

[4] Dallas Willard, *The Divine Conspiracy* (HarperCollins, 1998)

the ultimate Architect of grace, are they so graceless, so negative, and so addicted to spiritualised snooping and finding fault? Ironically, for some their spirituality has been a toxic force that has affected them for the negative; they are the worse for their praying. Extended prayer is not an automatic guarantee of anything, actually. It didn't produce any positive character transformation in the lives of the Pharisees. Prayer that is *practised* but not *connected* can actually corrupt; giving us a sense of self-accomplishment that is hugely deceptive. Our supposed 'proficiency' in the area of prayer can blind us to huge faults in other areas of our lives. This blindness comes because we view prayer as a profoundly *spiritual* activity; therefore we reason that we must be spiritual because we pray, even if we are a disaster in other areas. But to be proficient in prayer is not necessarily to be proficient at being Christian. Sometimes there are other, more telling indicators.

D.T. Niles told a story of negative piety when he addressed Princeton University

Sometime after World War II, during the reconstruction of Europe, the World Council of Churches wanted to see how its money was being spent in some remote parts of the Balkan Peninsula. Accordingly it dispatched John Mackie, who was then the president of the Church of Scotland, and two brothers in the cloth of another denomination – a rather severe and pietistic denomination – to take a jeep and travel to some of the villages where the funds were being disbursed.

One afternoon Dr. Mackie and the other two clergymen went to call on the Orthodox priest in a small Greek village. The priest was overjoyed to see them, and was eager to pay his respects. Immediately, he produced a box of Havana cigars, a great treasure in those days, and offered each of his guests a cigar. Dr. Mackie took one; bit the end off, lit it, puffed a few puffs, and said how good it was. The other gentlemen looked horrified and said, 'No, thank you, we don't smoke.'

Realising he had somehow offended the two who refused, the priest was anxious to make amends. So he excused himself and reappeared in a few minutes with a flagon of his choicest wine. Dr. Mackie took a glassful, sniffed it like a connoisseur, sipped it and praised its quality. Soon he asked for another glass. His companions, however, drew themselves back even more noticeably than before and said, 'No, thank you, we don't drink!'

Later, when the three men were in the jeep again, making their way up the rough road out of the village, the two pious clergymen turned upon Dr. Mackie with a vengeance. 'Dr. Mackie,' they insisted, 'do you mean to tell us that you are the president of the Church of Scotland and an officer of the World Council of Churches and you smoke and drink?'

Dr. Mackie had had all he could take, and his Scottish temper got the better of him. 'No, dammit, I don't,' he said, 'but somebody had to be a Christian!'[5]

Piety, if it is not truly Jesus-centred, can poison.

An irony: spirituality itself is heady, dangerous stuff

The poisoned chalice of pride is often offered to those who are more recognised for their praying. In recent years, it's become usual to describe a group of people with a special gifting in prayer as *intercessors*. At one level, it's reasonable to recognise and release people into

---

[5] Donald McCullough, *The Trivialization of God: The Dangerous Illusion of a Manageable Deity* (NavPress, 1995)

the gift and call that God gives. But, on the other hand, I'm a little nervous of this tagging of people; the 'intercessors' can begin to act like the Royal Marines of prayer, the crack troops of spiritual warfare, all-weather warriors who can penetrate areas of darkness hitherto unexplored by humankind...

Sometimes the intercessory gift is genuine – but gets hijacked. I can think of a church right now where the intercessors are causing all kinds of grief, demanding to know details of just who in the church is going through marriage problems, where there are struggles with teenagers – because they and they alone have the keys for breakthrough in these areas of difficulty. A critical attitude can easily settle on the landing strip of the intercessor. Because they have a genuine radar perception, God shares 'intelligence' information with them on a real 'need to know' basis. But if that intelligence is not used solely as a fuel for prayer, a critical attitude is waiting to envelope them.

I remember seeing this in action when living in a small community in southern Oregon, USA. A number of the men in the church had developed a burden for prayer that was authentic and committed. They were gathering together at 4am every day at the church building. Sounds good? It was – for a while. But here's how the 'lead intercessor' announced the meetings over a series of Sunday mornings...

Week one: the leader of the prayer group walks quietly to the pulpit, a broad, excited grin on his face, his eyes sparkling with real joy.

'A few of us are feeling that God is asking us to pray every day for this community. We've had a wonderful week as we've got together each morning, and I'd like to invite you all to come and be a part of it. We meet at 4am in the prayer room – hope to see you there...'

Week two: the same leader, his face now wreathed in a weaker smile, and his shoulders slightly hunched from sheer tiredness, walks slowly to the pulpit.

His voice has a weary drone. 'This week, a few people who are responding faithfully to a call to sacrificial prayer have been braving the early morning cold to come out and pray for this community that is lost and is in great darkness. We could use your help too. Hope to see you tomorrow morning at 4am…'

Week three: slowly the same prayer leader, close to total exhaustion now, blinks wearily at the congregation. There is no smile now, and his eyes are slightly glazed. Tinges of blue can be seen in the bags beneath those eyes. He is mildly angry.

'Yet again, the needs of this community are being borne upon the shoulders of a remnant of this church, a small, but mighty group who are sick to death of insipid, lukewarm Christianity, and who are valiantly continuing the spiritual warfare that is needed if this wretched community is to be saved. Are there others here who will reject the kind of half-heartedness that makes Jesus vomit? See you tomorrow, I hope…'

Week four (the last week that the *few* gathered): the prayer leader now looks like Lazarus – before Jesus passed by. He can barely string two sentences together, and he is enraged with the white-hot poker passion of the incensed zealot. His eyelids droop their testimony to his state of sleep deprivation, but they shroud eyes that still blaze with anger. His voice trembles as he speaks, barely able to contain his incensed indignation:

'Does anyone around here really care at all? Does anyone really believe the Bibles that we hold in our hands today? God will surely judge the pathetic backslidden hearts of all of us.' He looks around the building with a suddenly alert, piercing gaze, searching out non-praying people for a lightning bolt. He continues, his voice slowly, methodically passing sentence, like a judge with black cap passing down the sentence of the hangman's noose to a crowd of hapless criminals: 'This will be our last week of special prayer. Come and join us if you can be bothered... and may the Lord have mercy upon your souls...'

Not many people turned out to pray that week. The otherwise nice chap had been turned into a gibbering religious ranter. The passionate pursuit of God had been tragically hijacked by cynicism and disappointment. Of course, extended prayer is a discipline that is vital – but beware the hijacking of even the purest forms of spiritual aspiration.

Ready to forgive: help, there are humans around here...

We are called to forgive as part of the act of prayer and it can seem like an Everest to climb. Our struggle to forgive is sometimes rooted in the surprise that we feel that we might actually have to. We can develop a completely unrealistic set of expectations, particularly when it comes to our churches. Someone came to me recently and announced in hushed and stunned whispers that they had discovered that their church had some weaknesses! One would think that this would come as no surprise, and that to reach this rather obvious conclusion was not exactly rocket science, but we can forget that we are ourselves basically human – and therefore prone to sin, mistakes, false motives, loud mouths, impurity, thoughtlessness, and a host of other maladies associated with the human condition. And, in the church, we are still hemmed in by... humans. Like ourselves. But we want to forget this, and live in a Utopia where all is sweetness and light. Beware: disappointment is just around the corner.

I occasionally encounter this 'He's more than human, you know' attitude when I turn up as a guest speaker at a church service. The prayer time beforehand can be utterly terrifying. Genuinely kind people gather around me, massage my shoulders, shout in my ear and spit in my face, and ask the Lord to heal the sick, cast out demons, and raise the dead, if indeed there are any of the departed present, during the service and through little *me*, the hapless guest speaker.

And I'm not alone in being elevated to superhuman status; people often do this to church leaders generally. However, if they then make a mistake, take a wrong turn, or change the service time (an usually dangerous decision) and the numbers go down by six as a result of it, then look out... there are always those whose pastoral response to any kind of error from leadership, no matter how small, is to yell, 'Burn the witch!'

The command of Jesus is clear: we've been shown much, much grace. So let's pass it around, lest – to paraphrase that little story about the unjust servant – we who have been forgiven a lottery sized list of transgressions take up accountancy and meticulous audit everybody else's overdraft.

Grace requires compromise

I occasionally wish that there was a Bible verse that said 'Lighten up, sayeth the Lord', or alternatively,

'Chill, my people.' We Christians can be people of such principle that we don't know when to relax, and we end up majoring on minors, and when that happens, grace is always the first casualty. 'Here I stand, I can do no other' we cry, Martin Luther style, in the bold spirit of the Reformation, as we protest about the proposal to change the hymnbooks, or, God forbid, move the piano from the left side of the church to the right side. And worse still, we name God in our protests, insisting that he is surely as aggrieved as we are. Of course, deep down we know the truth; God doesn't care where the piano is sited. Pack away the prayer meeting and stop fasting about *that* decision. Just stick the piano wherever. The difficulty is further compounded by our insistence in using spiritual language in our conflicts. We don't say, 'I don't like you'. No, our Christian code causes us to cry 'You have grieved my spirit.' What?

The use of the word 'compromise' in this heading may shock some, and I have chosen it deliberately. Jesus compromised all the time in his daily walk with his friends and disciples. Couldn't he have spent all day, every day listing their faults and weaknesses? But he did not. And he wrote to two of the seven churches of Revelation 1-3 and found absolutely no fault with them whatsoever. Does that mean that they were flawless and without any hint of weakness? Of course not, but it does mean that while Jesus is perfect, he isn't picky, crusading about every single issue of weakness and jumping on every mistake. What an irony: those who have been showered with amazing grace, running around with microscopes and magnifying glasses in search for sin, desperately hunting down and exposing everybody else's shortcomings.

Misunderstandings about forgiveness

In praying about forgiving others, we are not merely
stating an intention or vowing to forgive: we are asking
for help in what is often a very difficult act. People are
damaged when they are told just to forgive in some kind
of offhand way; the abused are made to feel that they are
guilty because of the right anger that they feel; a new
abuse. Indeed, we Christians don't do well with anger;
we're nervous of it, because it isn't tidy or nice. But a
woman who has been raped has every right to feel very
angry; and a quick prayer renouncing those agonising
emotions will not fix everything; indeed, it may cause
further damage.

Forgiveness is not an act that seeks to pretend that
what was done to us was not wrong; on the contrary, the
very fact that it is *forgiveness* that is offered clearly recognises that sin has indeed been committed; to state the
obvious, if it wasn't wrong, then it does not need to be
forgiven. Forgiveness does not bless sin. Nor does
forgiveness release the other party from the negative
consequences of their actions. Everything may not return
as it was; indeed, some relationships may be fractured
beyond repair. Forgiveness does not imply that there will
actually be full reconciliation. The damage done to a
marriage shattered by adultery may be an example; the
aggrieved party may indeed forgive, but that does not
necessarily mean that the marriage will continue.
Scripture seems to give the wounded party a choice
about that. In just the same way that we can be forgiven
by God for our follies, yet may still suffer the natural
consequences of them, so forgiveness doesn't cancel out
the effect that our sin has caused.

I believe that forgiveness has little to do with feelings;
again, it may be that our emotions are screaming with

indignation, and itching for vengeance. Forgiveness is a choice that says that we will end our self-appointed role as the avenger; rather, I will, by God's help, hand the situation and the person over to God.

Forgiveness and prayer

Bitterness is a consuming force, fuelled by the power of obsession. It can fill our waking moments and our dreams at night. And it really makes the possibility of a single-minded pursuit of God in prayer very unlikely, as it robs me of my energy and clutters my heart and brain with dark, but mostly vain and impotent thoughts. It will destroy my ability to pray for others; bitterness is not a targeted, laser-like emotion that is specific, but a clumsy, omni-directional force that spills over and sours all our relationships. We can hardly pray that the kingdom will come in the world when our own hearts are wrestling to be the God of Justice – or more likely, injustice, in our own theatres of relational war. And our wrestling goes on and on and on, and causes untold damage – particularly in the church, which is why the writer to the Hebrews was adamant

> See to it that no one misses the grace of God and that no bitter root grows up to cause trouble and defile many...[6]

Myra Hindley was the other half of one of the most infamous and hated couples of contemporary criminal history. Together with her lover, Ian Brady, Hindley subjected young children to unspeakable sexual abuse and torture before killing them in what became known as the

---

[6] Hebrews 12:15

Moors Murders. The British public was outraged when, at their trial, a recording that this evil pair had taped, that of one of their young victims, was played. The distraught parents in the public gallery had to listen to the haunting sounds of their beloved child sobbing, begging for mercy and pleading for Mum. The nation felt a fury that has raged and blazed unabated.

The fire still burns. Hindley recently died in prison; the police were forced to mount a special guard on her body lest, even in death, she become the target for vengeance, a vengeance that she was obviously beyond. And the sadness is that more lives have been lost than those innocent children in the bleak nights on the moors long ago: parents and relatives have spent their whole lives on a journey of unrequited hatred, a further tragic waste, a never-ending hunt for a payback that never really came. Even if they had been able to get their hands around the necks of this terrible pair, it would not have brought satisfaction.

And I shrink back from what I have just written, knowing too well that I know nothing of the awful, gut-wrenching pain and loss that they felt. No wonder forgiveness, whatever it pardons, can only come as a result of heaven's help. But I can point to one who has been to a similar hell – and back.

Imagine this scene from a recent courtroom trial in South Africa:

A frail black woman stands slowly to her feet. She is something over seventy years of age. Facing her from across the room are several white security police officers, one of whom, Mr Van der Broek, has just been tried and found implicated in the murders of both the woman's son and her husband some years before. It was indeed Mr Van der Broek, it has now been established, who had come to the woman's home a number of years back, taken her son, shot him at point-blank range and then burned the young man's body on a fire while he and his officers partied nearby.

Several years later, Van der Broek and his cohorts had returned to take away her husband as well. For many months she heard nothing of his whereabouts. Then, almost two years after her husband's disappearance, Van der Broek came back to fetch the woman herself. How vividly she remembers that evening, going down to a place beside a river where she was shown her husband, bound and beaten, but still strong in spirit, lying on a pile of wood. The last words she heard from his lips as the officers poured gasoline over his body and set him aflame were, 'Father, forgive them.'

And now the woman stands in the courtroom and listens to the confessions offered by Mr Van der Broek. A member of South Africa's Truth and Reconciliation Commission turns to her and asks, 'So what do you want? How should justice be done to this man who has so brutally destroyed your family?'

'I want three things,' begins the old woman calmly, but confidently. 'I want first to be taken to the place where my husband's body was burned so that I can gather up the dust and give his remains a decent burial.'

She pauses, then continues. 'My husband and son were my only family. I want, secondly, therefore, for Mr Van der Broek to become my son. I would like for him to come twice a month to the ghetto and spend a day with me so that I can pour out on him whatever love I still have remaining within me.'

'And finally,' she says, 'I want a third thing. I would like Mr Van der Broek to know that I offer him my forgiveness because Jesus Christ died to forgive. This was also the wish of my husband. And so, I would kindly ask someone to come to my side and lead me across this courtroom so that

I can take Mr Van der Broek in my arms, embrace him and let him know that he is truly forgiven.'

As the court assistants come to lead the elderly woman across the room, Mr Van der Broek, overwhelmed by what he has just heard, faints. And as he does, those in the court-room, friends, family, neighbours – all victims of decades of oppression and injustice – begin to sing, softly, but assuredly, 'Amazing grace, how sweet the sound, that saved a wretch like me.'[7]

Grace at the heart of it all

Perhaps day-to-day forgiveness is fuelled by the know-ledge that not only are we all human, but as Christians, we are part of the community of the con-demned-but-now-pardoned. Charles Colson tells of visiting a prison in the city of Sao Jose dos Campos, one that was turned over to two Christians twenty years ago

> They called it Humaita, and their plan was to run it on Christian principles. The prison has only two full-time staff; the rest of the work is done by inmates. Every prisoner is assigned another inmate to whom he is accountable. In addition, every prisoner is assigned a volunteer family from the outside that works with him during his term and after his release. Every prisoner joins a chapel program, or else takes a course in character formation.
>
> When I visited Humaita, I found the inmates smiling – particularly the murderer who held the keys, opened the gates, and let me in. Wherever I walked I saw men at peace. I saw clean living areas, people working industriously. The walls were decorated with biblical sayings from Psalms and

---

[7] Source unknown

Proverbs. Humaita has an astonishing record. Its recidivism rate is 4 percent compared to 75 percent in the rest of Brazil and the United States. How is all this possible?

I saw the answer when my guide escorted me to the notorious punishment cell once used for torture. Today, he told me, that block houses only a single inmate. As we reached the end of a long concrete corridor and he put the key into the lock, he paused and asked, 'Are you sure you want to go in?'

'Of course,' I replied impatiently. 'I've been in isolation cells all over the world.' Slowly he swung open the massive door, and I saw the prisoner in that punishment cell: a crucifix, beautifully carved by the Humaita inmates – the prisoner Jesus hanging on the cross.

'He's doing time for all the rest of us,' my guide said softly.

9

Only come to God in the summer season...

Lead us not into temptation, and deliver us from evil...

Troubles come...

A story is told of a policeman who was seeking promotion to Sergeant, and so was taking a test paper. In the course of the examination he found a question focused on decision making and ordering priorities. The question read

> You are driving along a road in your patrol car, when suddenly a car coming from the other direction veers across the road and smashes into another car. As you approach the first car, you notice the wife of the police inspector who is in charge of your station is driving it, and that a very strong smell of alcohol is coming from her car. You look into the *other* car, and notice that a well-known local criminal and thief, who has jumped bail and is on the run, is driving that car, and he is sitting there looking dazed. In the back of his car are boxes of video recorders. Just then a tanker, trying to avoid the two cars, veers off the road and ploughs

into some shop fronts. The tanker driver, distraught, jumps out of the cab, and comes running towards you yelling 'Fire! fire! *Do* something, officer!!', and then you notice that the words 'Toxic waste – High explosive' are marked on the side of the tanker. Just then a gang of twenty-five large chaps who just happened to be passing begin looting the shop, which has now caught fire. *Please list your priorities and decisions...*

The policeman taking the test paper gave this precise answer. 'Priority and decision number 1. Remove uniform and mingle with crowd.'

I'm with him. I don't like trouble, and used to feel guilty about that because I thought I was supposed to greet trial and difficulty with a sense of breathless, thrilled excitement.

Oh, deep and prevailing joy! I have the flu today, my ears are so bunged up that I feel like I'm twenty fathoms beneath water, my nose is dripping like a terminally damaged tap, and I have the inestimable privilege of walking through my day with two rather large menthol inhalers stuck up my nostrils. What blessedness is this? How shall my faith grow as a result, I wonder?

Scripture seems to instruct us to be glad *in* trials, because with God, nothing is wasted. His grace is mine, his presence is sure (flu or no flu) and he has the knack of bringing something good out of something bad, like a stronger faith. But that doesn't mean that I've got to pretend that I like it, or wander down the street just hoping that a lorry will drive over my foot, just the thing to help refine my ability to rejoice in tribulation. When it comes to bad stuff happening to good people (or even me), I want to join the aforementioned constable: remove uniform and mingle with crowd – in other words, get away from the source of hassle as quickly as possible.

I like bright, sunny, balmy days, filled with laughter, friendship, love and good wine. Sadly, we are not promised only days of this sort – indeed the opposite. Jesus did actually promise us that we would have trouble in this world[1] – not my favourite text and certainly not one that I've got stuck to my refrigerator door.

And here we are taught to pray about temptation and evil – which is not primarily about temptation to sin, although that's part of it. More specifically, it is a prayer that we might not face trials of many kinds. But before we think about this in relationship to prayer, let's face the stone cold, unpalatable fact – suffering *will* touch us all in some way in this life. It is unavoidable. No amount of pretending, super-faith or ultra triumphal talk will change that.

A lady went to one of those churches where suffering wasn't allowed. No one admitted to having any problems at all, to do so would be a 'negative confession' and evidence of a lack of faith. Her husband, who was unwell, did not accompany her to the service. Noticing this, one of the leaders launched into a little pastoral interrogation: 'Where's your husband?' he asked. She was honest, and said it like it was: 'He's sick.'

The reply was swift and sure from the leader: 'He is not sick. Christians don't get sick. He just *thinks* he's sick.'

'Thank you,' she replied. 'I'll go home and tell him.'

The next week she came back without him again. Once again, the leader was intrigued: 'Where's your husband?' The reply was more intriguing: 'Well, he thinks he's dead.' Whether the above actually happened, I have no clue. But it does illustrate the reality that sickness and death are part of the deal for us earthlings; Christians and all.

---

[1] John 16:33

A quick bit about suffering[2]

Nowhere does Scripture suggest that Christians will experience freedom from suffering – on the contrary, the Bible makes it very clear that suffering and trials are a very likely part of the life of faith.

In Old Testament terms, the Hebrews had a fairly straightforward view on suffering: sinners suffer. They regarded suffering as punishment for sin against God's moral order. The wicked would surely suffer because of their evil ways[3] even though they might prosper for a time.[4] In fact, some writers express consternation and frustration that God had *not* lifted a hand of judgment against the offenders of his will.[5] They often quickly interpreted their own suffering as a sign of God's punishment for sin in their lives. The highly developed sense of corporate identity in Hebrew thought meant that it was believed that suffering could come as a result of parents' sin;[6] an idea reflected by Jesus' disciples in the story of the healing of the man born blind[7] or the wickedness of the king.[8] But there was a big problem with this way of thinking – what about the suffering of the righteous? This was explained variously as a way for God to gain people's attention[9] or to develop or refine character.[10] Ultimately, the writers

---

[2] Some of this material is adapted from T.R. McNeal Holmans Bible Dictionary

[3] Psalms 7:15,16; 37:1–2; 73:12-20; 139:19

[4] Job 21:28-33

[5] Jeremiah 12:1-4; Habakkuk 1:2-4; Malachi 3:7-15

[6] Ezekiel 18

[7] John 9:2

[8] 1 Kings 21:20,22,29

[9] Job 33:14; 36:15

[10] Job 23:10; Psalm 66:10

consigned themselves to trust in God's sometimes hidden wisdom: they were content with mystery.[11]

Check out the lives of the New Testament Christians and you'll see that pain was very much part of their daily experience.[12] Our long-suffering ancestors tasted *tribulation* – the Greek word means pressure; and in classical Greek it is always used in its literal sense. It is used, for instance, to describe the plight of a man who was tortured to death by being slowly crushed by a great boulder laid upon his chest. Some of my readers know that feeling right now, even as you turn this page; the rock that you carry of that sickness, that anxious fear for your wayward prodigal, that financial burden that just won't go away; the rock sits upon your chest, threatening, at times, to crush the very life out of you. As I write this, I feel the weight of a rock that has been sitting on me for the last year or so. It would be inappropriate and self-pitying to lay the details of my own stonework on you, my reader. Compared with what some of you carry, my stone is a mere pebble. But know that I am not just writing from the *Happytown* place of theory. Some days my rock eclipses my view of God – I can barely squint around it to get any view of him at all. And at other times, the weight of it makes me breathless, and tempts me to feel that I can't do anything at all useful today – I have neither the faith nor the energy. And yet other days are days of guilt: shouldn't mountains – and therefore rocks, which are bits of mountains – be the stuff that I'm supposed to hurtle into the sea with just the tiniest speck of faith? The rock remains, and I feel hope, despair, and in turn, qualification to teach and preach (I'm part of the fellowship of the rock) and then disqualification

---

[11] Job 42:2,3; Psalm 135:6

[12] 2 Corinthians 1:6, 8:2; Philippians 1:29; James 1:12; 1 Peter 1:6, 3:14, 4:122

(what right have I got to say anything with this huge boulder – or so it looks to me – sitting on me?)

As well as tribulation, the early Christians often suffered *poverty* as well, and in many cases were described as being destitute, having nothing of worth at all. Generally speaking, the early Christians were poor.[13] This carried not only the obvious burden of caring for your family and yourself, but also a huge social stigma was attached to having little. Roman thinking suggested that to be poor meant that you were of absolutely no consequence. The poverty of the Christians may have come from a combination of their background prior to coming to Christ, coupled with hardship following their conversion, perhaps because their homes were plundered.[14]

And then, if all of this was not bad enough, the early Christians were *slandered* and maligned, and accused of the most appalling crimes. Perfectly innocent ideas, like the brotherhood and sisterhood of believers, and the Eucharist, were twisted and made to sound as if incest and cannibalism were common practice among the 'Nazarenes'. Talk of loving one's 'brother or sister' and of eating Christ's body and drinking his blood was used to fuel the slander.

The early Christians recognised the inevitability of their suffering. As Christ suffered, so would they.[15] Continuing his mission, they would incur tribulation[16] because the world hates the disciples as much as it did their Lord.[17] Suffering for his sake was counted as a privilege. New Testament writers saw that trials were to be

---

13   1 Corinthians 1:26,27; James 2:5
14   Hebrews 10:34
15   John 16:33; Acts 14:22; Romans 8:31-39; 1 Corinthians 12:26;
     1 Thessalonians 2:14; 2 Timothy 3:12; 1 Peter 4:12,13
16   Mark 13:12,13
17   John 15:18; 1 Corinthians 2:8; 1 John 3:11-13

endured patiently rather than rebelliously[18] because
God was working his purpose out in his children's
lives.[19]

They certainly testified to the reality that none of us
want to admit – often those who have walked the hard-
est pathway are the most gracious and mature in their
faith, because faith can grow stronger through trials.[20]
In the darker days, we are driven back to the truth that
we will share Christ's ultimate triumph[21] the foretaste
of which is our experience of small, daily victories.[22]
Therefore, sufferings give birth to hope in us[23] and give
us a glimpse of the eternal horizon – no present suffering, the Bible teaches, compares with the rewards that
await the faithful follower of Christ.[24] And so... we will
suffer.

Our blinkered view of the world

All over the world, Christians suffer. That's reality for
many of us; thousands die for their faith every year,
while others get ill, lose those they love, and so on. But
then following Jesus was never supposed to be an easy
life – why else would he have said 'Take up your cross
and follow me?'

---

[18]　1 Thessalonians 3:3; James 1:2-4
[19]　Romans 8:28,29
[20]　Hebrews 12:11; 1 Peter 4:1
[21]　Mark 13:9; John 16:33; 2 Thessalonians 1:5
[22]　Romans 8:37; 1 Peter 5:10; 1 John 2:13,14
[23]　Romans 12:12
[24]　Romans 8:17,18

Yet prayer still asks for us to be delivered from trials...

Why don't we want trials? Mainly, I suggest, because we don't trust our ability to cope with them well. Not with-standing the truth that faith can become like gold in the furnace of trial, that still doesn't mean that I have to yell, 'Bring 'em on!'

Jesus was once assailed[25] by a couple of his friends (who had brought their mother along for added weight) and asked to be given special thrones of honour. In responding, he asked them whether they would be able to 'drink the cup that he was going to drink' – the cup of suffering, typified by the Gethsemane experience. They, full of a groundless but heady self-confidence, res-ponded that they were ready for the cup – a ludicrous assertion in retrospect, considering that when Calvary day finally rolled up, they all ran away.

James and John *would* one day sip from suffering's unwelcome cup – one day John would be exiled in Patmos, and James would be martyred on a whim by Herod. But in the meantime, they forgot who they were. And Peter also overestimated his own capacity for trial, asserting he would never deny Christ – even if every-body else would. I think that I can happily pray that I might be spared days of trial, if at all possible. I think I can trust God for them, but I just don't trust *me*.

...and prayer is devil aware

Trials aren't sin – but the time of trial is often the time when we are tempted to sin; Satan would tempt

---

[25] Matthew 20:20

believers to be defeated in their seasons of suffering.[26] Obviously, God does not 'lead us' into temptation – God cannot tempt us with evil so there is no need for us to ask him not to when his word assures us that he won't![27] John Stott believes the best translation of this phrase is 'deliver us from the evil one' who of course is the tempter. The time of trial is often the time when the enemy would seek to establish a foothold in our lives, perhaps sowing seeds of bitterness and disappointment towards God.

We must pray for a balanced view of Satan; there are some who see the 'hand of the enemy' in every tiny calamity, many of which we are to blame for because of our negligence. Running out of petrol or catching a cold as a result of swimming in January is *not* the devil's fault. We messed up without his help. Yet others are loath to see life as any kind of battlefield at all, fearing an unhealthy preoccupation with the devil; and as they do, they miss the message of the last book of the Bible – behind the scenes, in the macro and the micro, a battle between good and evil rages.

More about praying on the dark days

As we come to the Father, 'in the heavens', we remind ourselves that we come to the God who not only knows our dark days but shares in our suffering. At the heart of Christianity is the cross: the symbol that forever reminds us that God has entered a suffering world, to suffer for us and with us. It is no mere cliché, but historical reality that, however deep our pain, he's been there, and is there with us now.

---

[26] 2 Corinthians 4:8-12; Revelation 2:10

[27] James 1:13-15

Of course, in affirming that the cross demonstrates that Christ has walked through pain and that therefore he knows what it is to walk with us in ours, we never lose sight of the truth that this is not just about identification. Just before Jesus died, he turned to the criminal at his side and *did not* say, 'I tell you the truth, today I am with you at Calvary' – that's empathy – but he *did* say, 'I tell you the truth, today you'll be with me in paradise.'

God does not just weep with us, but – through the work of the cross – is able to bring his power as well as his tears to our situation: Jesus is not just our sympathetic friend, he is our sympathetic high priest.[28] And the cross is far more than a love letter made of wood.

In dark days, we pray and remind ourselves that darkness does not mean that we have been deserted. In the library of Corpus Christi College, Cambridge, is a rather dirty-looking Bible which belonged to Thomas Bilney, one of the minor characters of the English Reformation in the sixteenth century. He was no great hero and sometimes wavered in his faith. But in the end he was burnt at the stake for his commitment to the gospel. In his Bible, the verses which comforted him in his last days (in his version, in Latin) are heavily marked in ink: 'Fear not, for I have redeemed you; I have summoned you by name; you are mine ... When you walk through the fire, you will not be burned; the flames will not set you ablaze. For I am the Lord, your God, the Holy One of Israel, your Saviour.'[29]

We can be quick to assume that the advent of pain and suffering in our lives suggests that God has become distant, or perhaps has even deserted us completely, abandoning us to our 'fate'. But although God is not the

---

[28] Hebrews 4:15

[29] Isaiah 43:1-3

author of our pain, he is fully aware of all that we face. We must remember this when we face pain or opposition.

I have not been as well equipped for dark days as I might, because I have not sufficiently valued and sought out the prayer support of others. Make it a practice to find out how you can pray for your friends and others – and let them know how they can pray for you. Don't hesitate! The Bible places a high value on our praying for those who suffer

> Remember those in prison as if you were their fellow prisoners, and those who are ill-treated as if you yourselves were suffering.[30]

And

> Carry each other's burdens, and in this way you will fulfil the law of Christ.[31]

And pray for endurance – an oft mentioned New Testament theme. As Stephen Travis says: 'Remember that, for most of us, the Christian life is a marathon race, not a sprint. There is no quick escape from hardship. There is what has been called "a long obedience in the same direction."'[32]

Being honest in prayer: Let me tell you about what it's like, God

I have had some wonderful times of prayer, which involved me telling God very clearly that I didn't like what

---

[30] Hebrews 13:3
[31] Galatians 6:2
[32] Stephen Travis, *You've Got Mail* (Carlisle: Spring Harvest/Authentic, 2002)

was going on. I see absolutely no merit in pretending or speechmaking: God knows what's in our hearts anyway, and he is able to cope with our protests. We make them in the knowledge that God is God, and therefore worthy of our respect and submission, and we do so knowing that we are looking at life from our vantage point, which is a billion miles below his – yet still we can be authentic. When Jesus cried, 'My God, my God, why have you forsaken me?'[33] he was doing more than reading a prophetic script (Messiah is supposed to quote Old Testament scriptures shortly before dying, so, here we go, 'My God...') Rather, he was sobbing out the agony of what he really felt at that moment – *and* fulfilling the oracles of old in being the rejected one. The most common prayers of the Psalmist are 'Why?' and 'How long?' We can join in the litany of reality too.

Back to 'Father' again – affirming our identity on the dark days

We tend to think of the agony of Calvary as being mainly physical and spiritual; but I suggest that there was an emotional tormenting going on there that centred around who Jesus was in his Sonship. Think on it; as he hangs there, he is at his lowest ebb, doing his greatest work – and the taunting voices shout a familiar question, cheer-led from hell

Who are you, Jesus?

Our spiritual identity is critical: Satan would wrest it from our grasp with the whisper

Who do you think you are?

---

[33] Matthew 27:46

which is why God shouts louder about identity in
Scripture

> But you are a chosen people, a royal priesthood, a holy
> nation, a people belonging to God, that you may declare the
> praises of him who called you out of darkness into his won-
> derful light. Once you were not a people, but now you are
> the people of God; once you had not received mercy, but
> now you have received mercy. [34]

These are not rosy platitudes from a Hallmark greeting
card God, or merely poetic sentimentality; they form that
backbone of who we are in Christ.

Luke describes three moments at the cross where the
cry went up in the face of Jesus himself: who do you
think you are?

– The rulers sneered: 'he saved others; let him save
himself *if he is* the Christ of God, the Chosen One.'

– The soldiers mocked: they offered him wine
vinegar and said, '*If you are* the king of the Jews, save
yourself.'

– And then one of the criminals who hung there
'hurled insults at him': '*Aren't you the Christ*? Save yourself and us!'

All three are singing off of the same satanic song sheet
– an attack on the jugular of Christ's identity. Of course,
this is just actually a repeat performance: it had been
played before at the beginning of Jesus' ministry, as he
was tempted in the wilderness. Again, it was three times
there that Satan hissed, 'if you are the Son of God...' And
so, at the beginning of his earthly ministry, Satan sought
to undermine the identity of Christ, which had been so
beautifully affirmed by the Father at his baptism, when

---

[34] 1 Peter 2:9

the voice declared, 'This is my beloved Son, whom I love.'

Watch a principle at work. In Luke 3, the Father affirmed the identity of Jesus. In Luke 4, Satan questions it. And then, at the *end* of his earthly ministry, affirmation and questioning takes place again. In his 22nd chapter, Luke alone records that an angel comforted Jesus in the garden of Gethsemane.[35] And then the various parasites gather at the cross, ready to suck the very life of Jesus out of him as they laid siege to his identity, three times again. But he will not be so mugged. Twice he yells out the family name: 'Father!'

Father forgive them, for they do not know what they are doing.[36]

Father into your hands I commit my spirit.[37]

Dark days conspire to make us lose sight of who we are: that we belong to God as his beloved children. Sometimes, the only prayer you can muster when the grey skies gather, is the sob, 'Father'. It is enough. It says, 'I am yours. I belong to you. My trial has not obscured the truth of who I am. Whatever I have lost, this I will not lose. I am yours. You are mine.'

Look up on the dark days

I've heard it said that too much preaching about etern-ity and heaven produces Christians who are 'too heavenly minded to be of any earthly use' – a phrase I've used

---

[35] Luke 22:43

[36] Luke 23:34

[37] Luke 23:46

myself. But I wonder: has the pendulum swung yet again, causing us to lose sight of the incredible future before us? Compared with the vista of eternity, the New Testament writers were able to see the trials of this life in the context of being 'momentary',[38] as part of a life that is a 'mist that appears for a little while and then vanishes.'[39] Christ's coming will be in 'just a little while.'[40] Paul struggled with a genuine dilemma between remaining on earth to continue his ministry, or departing to be with Christ forever.[41] Eternity loomed large in the thinking of the early Christians.

Sometimes, all you have is the future. And it is hope that takes you through. There was much of this in the life and death of Jesus, who 'for the joy set before him endured the cross, scorning its shame, and sat down at the right hand of the throne of God.'[42]

One day the half sight of prayer will be over. Our struggling to peer through the fog will end, banished by the clear sunrise of his appearing. Prayer, as we have known it, will be abandoned, an out-of-date apparatus that saw us through the mists, but will be unnecessary now that we are fully at home with the Father. And so.....'we will be with the Lord for ever. Therefore encourage each other with these words.'[43] In the meantime, we often find ourselves in the swirling mists.

As I come to conclude this book, I find myself in another fog. This morning's banner headlines scream the news that policeman Stephen Oake, a father of three

---

[38] 2 Corinthians 4:17
[39] James 4:14
[40] Hebrews 10:37
[41] Philippians 1:21
[42] Hebrews 12:2
[43] 1 Thessalonians 4:17 and 18

from Manchester, was stabbed to death by some suspected terrorists just last night. Stephen, a much beloved and respected Christian, was a member of Poynton Baptist Church. I was speaking at the Mainstream conference, a gathering of around four hundred Baptists, when the news came through.

Kay and I have a great love for the Poynton crowd, some of whom were there at the conference, and we have shared a long-term friendship with their senior leaders, Rob and Marion White. We were due to leave at 10pm to drive to Heathrow to stay overnight and then board the plane in which I am now seated, tapping away these final reflections. But, perhaps madly, we lingered with a few of the Poynton people, wanting to savour our final moments of laughter and fun with these warm, animated lovers of God. We knew that we wouldn't get to the airport until 2am, but these people are worth the late night drive.

My friend Mark Elder came into the room, as we sat there, glasses of wine in hand, enjoying the ambience of a joyous evening. His announcement, made through eyes clouded with tears, stopped us in our tracks, as he told us that dear Stephen was the victim of murder. Waves of shock rippled around the room and for a moment, Kay and I felt that perhaps we should not be there at this time, intruders on their grief. And then, after the briefest moment, one by one, we just began to sob out prayers to God. Desperate, urgent, inarticulate, emergency prayers; stumbling intercessions for Stephen's family, now brutally robbed of a husband and father; heartfelt requests for wisdom for Rob and Marion as they were on their way back, even then, to try and minister and bring comfort in this darkest of nights. One or two prayers never ended with a formal *Amen*; the tears were their signal of conclusion.

Today, just twenty-four hours later, I see that we were in a profound moment of kingdom reality last night. An evening of laughter and fun, wine and stories, suddenly mingled with tears and anguish and questioning and heartbreak. The kingdom here, touching our lives with the vintage wine of friendship and reality, yet placed in a real world where the enemy of us all is still rampaging in his killing, stealing, destroying missions. Sometimes we raise our glasses in the midst of a fog bank. And even as I share this moment with you, I would ask you to remember Stephen's family in your prayers. By the time these words have become a book, the headlines will have faded; but we can still remember and ask that God might kiss them with his tender grace; even at this moment, as your eyes scan these words, will you whisper a request for them?

Light shines in the midst of darkness; the gold of heaven's king nestles in the dirt of a messed up, bloody world. The future is bright – yet we live in the *meantime*. So, in that meantime, keep breathing your prayers. Shout the urgent ones. Whisper your worship. Keep pressing in – and remember – prayer is for the fallen ones, like me, like you.

Thanks for taking this brief journey with me. Can we pray together before you go?

Join me in this paraphrase of the prayer of Clement of Rome, a contemporary of John the Apostle

> Open our inward eyes to recognise you, even though you are the highest in high heaven, the Holy One among the ranks of all the holy.
> You, Lord God, bring down the proud and outwit the cunning.
> You promote the humble and make the arrogant fall.
> You hold in your hand every issue of life: whether we are to be poor or rich, whether we are to live or to die.

You see every spirit, good or evil, and read the inmost
thoughts and intentions of every heart.

When we are in danger, you come to our aid.

When we are feeling desperate, you save us from our sense
of failure.

When events in the world overshadow us, help us to
remember who you are: the Creator and Overseer of
every living being.

Amen[44]

And... may God bless you.

---

[44] Adapted from David Winter, *After the Gospels* (Oxford: Bible
Reading Fellowship, 2001)

Equipping Christians to live actively, biblically and wholeheartedly for Christ — that's the goal of all that Spring Harvest does.

The Main Event

The largest Christian event of its kind in Europe — an Easter-time gathering of over 60,000 people for learning, worship and fun. The programme includes varied and inspiring choices for everyone, no matter how old or young, and no matter where you are in your Christian life.

Resources

- *Books* to help you understand issues that matter — prayer, family issues, Bible themes, workplace and more
- *Music albums* introducing new songs and showcasing live worship from the Main Event each year
- *Childrens resources* including popular music albums and songbooks
- *Songbooks* to introduce the best new worship material each year
- *Audio tapes* of teaching from Spring Harvest — a selection of thousands is available to choose from
- *Youth pastoral resources, songwords projection software, video services and more...*

Conferences

- *Youthwork the conference* — for volunteer youth workers, run in partnership with Youthwork magazine, YFC, Oasis Youth Action and the Salvation Army

- *At Work Together* to equip workers to effectively live and witness for Christ in today's challenging workplace.

Le Pas Opton is a beautiful four star holiday site on the French Vendée coast, exclusively owned and operated by Spring Harvest. Mobile homes, tents or your own tent/tourer — take your choice at this delightful resort where you'll find top quality facilities and excellent service.

Our aim at *Le Pas Opton* is to give you the opportunity for relaxation and refreshment of body, mind and spirit. Call Spring Harvest Holidays on 0870 060 3322 for a free brochure.

For more information contact our Customer Service team on 01825 769000 or visit our website at www.springharvest.org

Spring Harvest. A Registered Charity.

INVESTOR IN PEOPLE